Mentally Calm, Spiritually Connected

The Interdependence
of Mind and Spirit

Scott R. Frazer, PhD

CFI
An imprint of Cedar Fort, Inc.
Springville, Utah

© 2021 Scott R. Frazer
All rights reserved.

No part of this book may be reproduced in any form whatsoever, whether by graphic, visual, electronic, film, microfilm, tape recording, or any other means, without prior written permission of the publisher, except in the case of brief passages embodied in critical reviews and articles.

This is not an official publication of The Church of Jesus Christ of Latter-day Saints. The opinions and views expressed herein belong solely to the author and do not necessarily represent the opinions or views of Cedar Fort, Inc. Permission for the use of sources, graphics, and photos is also solely the responsibility of the author.

ISBN 13: 978-1-4621-3884-5

Published by CFI, an imprint of Cedar Fort, Inc.
2373 W. 700 S., Springville, UT, 84663
Distributed by Cedar Fort, Inc., www.cedarfort.com

Library of Congress Control Number: 2020952217

Cover design by Shawnda T. Craig
Cover design © 2021 Cedar Fort, Inc.

Printed in the United States of America

10 9 8 7 6 5 4 3 2 1

Printed on acid-free paper

Mentally Calm, Spiritually Connected

You can't really understand the importance of an event in history until you have a chance to look back on it and note its effect on your life. We didn't see the harm that COVID-19 could do to our spiritual lives until it hit. Churches, temples, and social interaction closed down. The months dragged by.

At any time, trying to understand and cope with one's mental and spiritual depression is a huge challenge, but it is especially true during this past year. Since you are reading these words and trying to understand yourself or others, I would like to dedicate this book to you. Your efforts are noteworthy. May God bless you in your efforts.

CONTENTS

ACKNOWLEDGMENTS..ix

PREFACE xi

CHAPTER 1
Mental & Spiritual Depression.. 1

CHAPTER 2
The Brain 19

CHAPTER 3
The Holy Ghost: One Voice among Many 35

CHAPTER 4
Mental Discipline and Decisions.. 39

CHAPTER 5
Neuroplasticity and Repentance 47

CHAPTER 6
The Physical, Mental, and Spiritual... 53

CHAPTER 7
Understanding the Heart Metaphor 61

CHAPTER 8
The Consciousness Conundrum.. 69

CHAPTER 9
The Soul and the Spirit 77

Contents

CHAPTER 10
Being Conscious of your Conscience..................................... 93

CHAPTER 11
Worry, Anxiety, and Fear... 107

CHAPTER 12
Drugs and Medications.. 117

CHAPTER 13
Sensory Addiction.. 125

CHAPTER 14
The Art of Meditation & Introspection 133

CHAPTER 15
Being Mindful of Your Mindedness............................. 141

CHAPTER 16
Scriptural Advice for Treating Depression 149

CHAPTER 17
A Healthy Brain Is Key to Eternal Life 157

EPILOGUE 165

ABOUT THE AUTHOR.. 167

viii

ACKNOWLEDGMENTS

I would first like to recognize the patience of my wife, Cheri, when I delay house chores "just to finish up this one thought" or when I'm late for dinner to "get this idea written down before I forget it." I'm sorry, my dear. Thoughts and ideas will abandon you if ignored for too long.

I wish to acknowledge the assistance of my publisher, Cedar Fort, for the counsel, motivation, direction, and deadlines to keep me on track.

I also wish to thank those who reviewed this book for me—Emma Gailey and Bill Hall. Finally, I want to acknowledge and thank my oldest son, Trent, who has been the first-read reviewer for all my books and has caused me more rewrites than anyone else. His suggestions have been invaluable.

PREFACE

You are a very complex entity, in ways only you can know. I am not talking about your physical body. Your doctor knows how your skeleton, tendons, and muscles interact to let you stand up, walk, or throw a ball. More specialized physicians understand how your organs do their jobs, although, as we will discuss, the brain is still rather a mystery.

The real complexity is in what you think and how you think it. You probably view yourself as being a single individual, with one mind and spirit. But the truth is that you are an association of your emotional mind, your rational thoughts, memories of experiences, and your spirit. Yet even that breakdown is too simplistic. Do you ever have just one emotion about a subject? Do you ever have just one thought about a quandary you are trying to resolve? How do your memories influence your opinions on your family, politics, and religion? What input do you get from your conscience about the morality of your actions? As you well know, you have multiple voices in your head at all times. Often those voices are at odds with one other.

We find this multiplicity of selves in the scriptures as well. In Mark 12:28, a scribe asked the Savior which is the first and greatest commandment. Two verses later, the Savior answered that he should love the Lord with all his heart, might, mind, and strength. Jesus based his response around Deuteronomy 6:5, which actually reads, "And thou shalt love the Lord thy God with all thine heart, and with all thy soul, and with all thy might," introducing yet another poorly defined concept called the soul into the mix. So, what exactly are your heart, might, mind, strength, and soul, and how do you focus them on loving the Lord? How do these components of the person that is you interact with one another? If one of these parts is broken, does it affect your ability to love the Lord?

xi

Preface

Most Christians, opting to prioritize their spiritual health, don't consider their mental health very often. At Church services, we tend to spend most of our time discussing our hearts and souls. We discuss spiritual health and what we can do to improve it. My youngest son once told me that if he was not paying attention in early morning seminary and a question was suddenly directed at him, he would rouse himself and answer, "Pray, read the scriptures, and obey the commandments." Nine times out of ten, he observed, it was the correct answer. Indeed, some form of the question "What should we do to improve our spirituality?" is very common in church instruction. This single-minded focus on spirituality is what we expect to hear in church, but it rather ignores the fact that our spirituality is very dependent on the health of our physical and mental selves.

In fact, your spiritual health is actually the lowest priority of your body and usually occurs only when your physical and mental states are stable. You probably know the consequences to your spirituality if your physical body is having problems. If you are sick with the flu or have just had knee surgery, spirituality is very difficult. Your brain is too caught up in the aches and pains of being ill or injured. The same is true if you are going through mental distress. If you have just lost your job, are grieving the death of a loved one, or are angry with someone, it is difficult to find peace and focus for effective prayer. In essence, you have to be physically and mentally right before presenting yourself to the Lord and hoping for inspiration.

Many people don't understand these limits on feeling the Spirit, so they get angry with the Lord. You may have even thought to yourself, "Here I am, going through a painful physical condition (or an overwhelming mental distress or emotional challenge), and God won't answer my prayers. Why am I not feeling the Spirit?" As we will discuss in a following chapter, your body, mind, and spirit are all connected. The point is that your body and brain must first attend to earthly demands and distractions before they can focus on seeking a spiritual experience. So, if a part of your mind or body is struggling, your worship of God will be negatively affected. The more control you have of your mental state and focus, the better your spiritual experiences will be.

To begin this discussion, I would like to talk to the person who lives right behind your forehead—also known as the conscious part of your brain. Obviously, I cannot talk to your whole brain. The subconscious

xii

Preface

part of your brain is much too busy keeping your heart beating, your lungs breathing, your stomach digesting, and other organs functioning to be bothered by a discussion about itself. That is why your subconscious mind is subconscious; it could be fatal if that part of your brain was ever distracted. So, I wish to address the conscious part of your brain—the part of you that observes the world through your eyes, hears the world through your ears, and feels the world through your skin. I want to talk to that entity who is reading these words, storing concepts in your memory, and deciding if this book is worth your time. Step out of yourself for a moment. It is a bit of a philosophical mystery how you can ask yourself the simple question, "What was I thinking?" Strangely, you have the ability to *use* your mind to *examine* your mind. It's a bit like gazing into a mirror to detect how your eyes see. As a fair warning, this book will continue to encourage your conscious mind to observe your own thoughts from the outside. It will encourage such introspection so you can more effectively consider your thought patterns, your conscious self, and your spirit.

As mental depression has made its way through our society, the more common question after introspection is, "Why am I feeling this way?" Indeed, depression is one of the fastest growing health issues facing our physicians today. For many people, depression remains a hidden mental condition because it can take months for a person to recognize the need for medical help. Part of that delay may be due to the paradox in the question, "If I can't tell why I'm feeling despondent, then who can?" To answer that question, again, your conscious mind needs to recognize that there is a problem and admit that you need help. Depression continues to rise at epidemic rates, though the causes of that increase are not well understood.

A seemingly unrelated trend is the fact that church attendance throughout the world is plummeting. Especially young people, even those once active in their churches, are abandoning their congregations all together. Polls confirm that fewer people are prioritizing prayer, Sabbath observance, or their own spirituality. This increasing *spiritual* depression is occurring at the same time as our *mental* depression. Given that our mental and spiritual states are so connected, would it be a surprise if the two types of depression were related? Could dealing with an increasingly busy and stressful world be causing mental despondency as well as spiritual disconnection? It seems very likely, as we will discuss in the following chapters.

Preface

To be very clear, this book should *not* be considered a replacement for medical help. I am not a licensed physician. Indeed, if you suspect that consulting with a therapist would help you to avert a mental crisis, then you should definitely do so.

The goal of this book is twofold. First, we will try to define the different parts of you that make up this complex entity of you. We will first try to examine your mental side, meaning your conscious mind, unconscious mind, and emotions (or "heart"). We will then try to define the words that describe your spiritual side, such as spirit, soul, and conscience. Second, we will discuss the complex relationship between your mind and your spirit and how they interact with one another.

In this increasingly social world of Facebook, Instagram, texts, and email, we have so many voices telling us what to do that it is getting harder to sort out our own thoughts or distinguish the whisperings of the Spirit. In the end, we need to understand that spiritual health requires good mental health, and mental health requires some effort. So, to the conscious mind of my reader, I would like to dedicate this book. God bless you in your journey.

CHAPTER 1

Mental and Spiritual Depression

As a world, COVID-19 caused a disruptive and traumatizing experience for nearly everyone. Fear of getting sick added to the anxiety of possibly losing a job or a business. Schools, businesses, and even churches were closed. We felt the isolation of social distancing combined with the distress of not being prepared if grocery stores ran out of food. We received continuous reports of the growing numbers of infections and deaths. This progression of disturbing news went on for weeks and filled us with a dread of what could happen next.

Depression, worry, and anxiety were increasing rather alarmingly long before the coronavirus made them worse. As a people in our busy, modern world, we had learned to deal with the normal challenges of earth life. But the coronavirus crisis was far from a normal demand, and its long-term effects have yet to be determined. Though most of us did enjoy some unexpected time at home with our families, the total effects of the coronavirus have not been positive. The entire population of the earth was frightened of the disease and the potential loss of jobs and income. So, how did you handle the stress? Have you suffered any long-term effects to your mental well-being?

Before you shrug and answer you are fine, how well do you know your own mind? Would you recognize a change in your thinking? I understand you live with your brain 24/7, but it doesn't mean you are well acquainted with it. You may portray yourself as an intelligent, capable individual with a bright future, but wonder internally how long you can keep this charade going. You may feel you have successfully attained your goals in life—and cannot fathom why you are so depressed that your doctor had to prescribe antidepressant medication for you. Or you may be worried about what's going on in the mind of a loved one. Watching your children struggle with the social pressures and demands of being teenagers can be heartbreaking. Watching your children continue to battle the discordant voices in their heads into adulthood is even harder. Prayer does not always work the way we hope. This often leads to frustration and even anger at Heavenly Father, as only He can understand your child's thinking. Most of us need to be strong supports for family, employers, God, and others. Thus, we feel the continuing need to "have our heads on straight." But in a busy world beset by COVID-19, that expectation is getting harder to meet.

A theme of this book is that we must be more concerned with maintaining a healthy brain to hope to be able to maintain a healthy spirit. People will spend hours each week working out at the gym to maintain a healthy physical body. But few people spend time addressing their mental health. In the last few decades, it seems life has become so much busier and complicated that our brains are struggling to keep up. The effects of neglecting to care for our minds are revealing themselves in unexpected ways.

Before we are able to address the question of how your mental state affects your spiritual state, we need to define some terms. To assess the health of your mind and spirit, you need to know something about them. Thus, there will be a chapter on the brain, with succeeding chapters discussing your heart, consciousness, soul/spirit, and conscience. What *is* your spirit exactly, and where does it reside? Out of all the thoughts in your head, which one is actually the Holy Spirit trying to communicate with you? The definitions of such words as *heart, spirit, soul, consciousness*, and *conscience* are actually hundreds of years old. An update of our definitions of these parts of ourselves is needed. Hopefully, we can then discover for ourselves and for those we love how to protect our minds and spirits from the assault of a new and noisy world.

Perhaps you feel a little self-conscious about introspection of any kind. If you were preparing to run a marathon, you would certainly work out to ensure that your physical body was up to the task. In this overly busy world, your brain runs its own version of a marathon nearly every day. So you should probably check on it occasionally. To get to a place of mental calm, you must know where mental calm is. This requires you to turn your thoughts inward and find out what drives your mind to make its decisions. "Know thyself" is an encouragement to understand your own mind, to know your strengths, admit your weaknesses, recognize your moods, and understand your temptations. All these characteristics reside and interact in your brain, so it is good to become familiar with them.

Today we are witnessing unprecedented mental and spiritual depression. We will discuss some of the possibilities believed to cause these distressing trends. This book will not try to psychoanalyze the reader in any way. But this book will try to define aspects of your mental and spiritual sides that you try to keep coordinated every day. If you better understand the parts of you and how they interact, maybe it will help you to manage the whole. To do that, however, we must define and describe your heart, might, conscious and unconscious minds, spirit, soul, and conscience. As a people, we are all struggling to deal with host of present-day challenges. To start our discussion, let's review some of the trends we are seeing in our society that reflect those struggles.

Depression

Depression is a generic term for a broad range of symptoms, only one of which is sadness. It is estimated that 350 million people are affected by depression worldwide.[1] In the United States, a 2016 survey found that 16.2 million adults had at least one depressive episode within the year.[2] The huge number of people who suffer from depression only adds to the frustration of trying to define it. Women are much more likely to suffer depression than men. Many people who are afflicted by depression have no idea why they are depressed. They often have beautiful homes, healthy families, and strong marriages. Why should they be depressed? There is nothing fundamentally different about the brain of someone dealing with depression and a person who is not. No brain scan, MRI, or EEG can diagnose depression. Exhibiting enough symptoms over a certain time period is the only way depression is diagnosed today. In any case, this rise in unexplained depression is a strong indicator of how critical it is to care for your own mental health.

Fortunately, medical researchers are learning more about depression every day. They have learned that depression is caused by numerous factors, everything from the organic chemistry that takes place in your neurons to how the different regions of your brain interact. Three specific brain segments appear to be most affected by depression. Three symptoms of depression—impulsivity, repetitive thoughts, and sensitivity to emotional events—originate in these three regions.[3] We know something about the problems in brain chemistry suffered during depression by observing the effectiveness of different medications. However, it is more difficult to determine what factors cause the brain to develop these malfunctions in the first place. The numerous definitions given for depression have added to the confusion of what it really is. The following quote seems to be one of the better descriptions I have read of clinical depression:

> People often think that depression is just being sad all the time, but it's far more than that. In fact, people with depression do not necessarily feel sad—they often feel numb, like an emptiness where emotion should be. Hopeless and helpless. Things that used to be enjoyable aren't fun anymore: food, friends, hobbies. Energy plummets. Everything feels different, and it's hard to explain why, because it shouldn't be.[3]

One's susceptibility to depression is often genetically inherited. If your parents suffered from depression, you have a greater likelihood of falling into it yourself. You can't, obviously, change your genetics. Susceptibility can also be increased by environment. If you had a difficult childhood, depression is a mental response that may manifest itself years later. Again, plainly, you cannot change your past. Specific hormone imbalances can contribute to depression so the health of your body can also add to your susceptibility. In summary, it is important to recognize that you can control only a few of the causes of depression, but it is equally important to do whatever you can, starting with pharmaceutical treatments and behavioral counseling.

Whether its original cause is genetic, environmental, or hormonal, depression is manifested by faulty chemistry in the brain. There is no shame in such a chemical imbalance. But a stigma still exists for many people. A book on depression by Mayo Clinic physicians summarizes this issue: "Many people avoid seeing a doctor because they mistakenly associate a diagnosis of depression with a failure of willpower or character. Although the stigma associated with mental illness is lessening, lack of knowledge, worry as to how others will react and concerns about confidentiality still keep people from seeking help."[4]

Associating depression with spiritual weakness has roots from millennia ago. Depression, better known as melancholia at the time, is mentioned in writings from Mesopotamia in the second century.[5] Melancholia was believed to be a spiritual malady rather than a physical condition.

Worse yet, it was believed to be caused by demonic possession, so priests, rather than physicians, tried to cure it. Consequently, depression was often treated with beatings, physical restraint, and starvation in attempts to drive the demons out. These theories and treatment continued through the Middle Ages. During the Age of Enlightenment of the eighteenth and nineteenth centuries, mental conditions came to be viewed as a weakness in temperament that could not be changed, so people with this condition were shunned or simply locked up. Since then, more advanced, though equally misguided treatments, were tried, including electrotherapy and lobotomies. Mercifully, in the 1950s, doctors noticed that a tuberculosis medication called isoniazid helped reduce depression in some people. This prompted further research into the use of drug therapies as a treatment for the condition. Pharmaceuticals and counseling became the standard therapy for depression, as it is today.

Depression is often measured by counting the number of people who suffer from a major depressive episode (MDE) in the course of a year. An MDE is defined as a period of two weeks or more of suffering symptoms of depression. The table below shows a significant increase in MDEs over seven years. From 2005 to 2011, depressive episodes were fairly constant. Then from 2011 to 2018, the numbers increased significantly for our younger generations (data from Substance Abuse and Mental Health Services Administration (SAMHSA); 2018 National Survey on Drug Use and Health).[6]

MAJOR DEPRESSIVE EPISODES BY AGE

AGE	AVE. MDES 2005—2011	MDEs 2018	% Change
12–17	8.2	14.4	**75.6**
18–25	8.3	13.8	**66.3**
26–49	7.6	8	5.3
over 50	4.9	4.5	-8.2

As might be expected from this data, prescriptions for antidepressants have skyrocketed in the past several years. Why has depression drastically increased in young adults from the ages of 12 to 25 but has remained comparatively unchanged for older adults?

The Days and Times of Depression

It has been suggested that mental and spiritual depression may be due to disturbing political issues that cause people to worry about the future of their world and families. Indeed, we live in politically turbulent times. But so have countless generations of the past. Social issues could hardly be considered novel to our latest two generations. The women's suffrage movement began in the mid-1800s under the leadership of Susan B. Anthony and others. The liberation of Blacks began with the American Civil War in 1861, and efforts to remove bigotry and racial prejudice from our government and culture has been going on steadily since then. In 1951, Harry Hay formed the Mattachine Society, the first national gay rights organization. The Daughters of Bilitis, the first national lesbian organization, was founded in 1956. Attendance at anti-Vietnam War protests of the 1960s were above and beyond anything we see today.

Granted, we do have more access to breaking news than we have ever had before. When I was a child, I remember news was shown on television at 6:00 p.m. and 10:00 p.m. That isn't so today, of course. With cable news and our active social media outlets, breaking news is available at any hour. But, even in those olden days, you could always pick up a newspaper and read the headline news, though the stories were a couple of days old. In reality, life is no more political today than it was in any other time in the past century. With news being broadcast so widely and repeatedly, it is easy to think that we live in exceptionally turbulent times. News items are picked up and broadcasted by dozens of news outlets and are then evaluated by experts and other pundits in hundreds of television, radio, and social media outlets. Anyone can add their opinion to the mix through Twitter, Instagram, or Snapchat—and millions of people do.

What major change in our society, mainly occurring in the first decade of the 2000s, precipitated such dramatic changes in select portions of our population? This is an easily answered question, of course. Computer technology exploded at the beginning of the new millennium. Not surprisingly, these new computer science innovations have mainly affected our younger generations, without significantly changing the habits of our older population. Increased depression in our younger generations appears well correlated with the explosion of computer technology and the Information Age.

The Internet, Social Media, and All That Comes with It

The World Wide Web became publicly available in 1991. Email started being sent on America Online and other internet service providers in 1995. But, for those who remember, the start of the Information Age was dial-up internet, which was both slow and cumbersome. Broadband internet gradually replaced dial-up, and by 2007 half of all internet users had made the switch.

The Internet (and our fascination with it) grew as new capabilities were introduced. Google was incorporated in 1998. Facebook became available to customers in 2004. Twitter was founded in 2006, and Instagram was launched in 2010.

Obviously, the correlation of depression with the introduction of the internet and social media has been noticed by many researchers. Hundreds of books and blogs are dedicated to decrying the effect of the media on our children. For a long time, it was thought that sitting close to a television screen was harmful. This concern has largely been put to rest. Nonetheless, screen time has been affecting us in ways we are just starting to uncover. Every person with a cell phone and computer should think about the time spent looking at an electronic screen as opposed to the real world around us. Obviously, our electronics bring significant knowledge, news, and information into our lives. The Information Age is truly a great time to be alive! In a mere moment, you can find out about any fact, news story, Hollywood rumor, or weather report for anywhere in the world. Thousands of video games are available for your diversion. You can keep in continuous contact with friends and family through your choice of messaging. Indeed, electronic technology has made our lives much easier . . . yet much busier.

Due to our cell phones, tablets, and laptops, our brain is besieged by an onslaught of messages from all over the world. Billions of email messages and texts are sent every hour. With Instagram, Facebook, and Twitter you can read multitudes of opinions from everyone you follow— and many others you don't. We are subjecting ourselves to so many voices that it appears that our brains are being overwhelmed. We are starting to see the physical consequences of all this mental busyness. Our brains are exhausted. But we persist, thinking the energy-draining effects will only be temporary. Even if we recognize the negative effects of our media binging, we cannot seem to stop. Knowing the dangers of texting while driving, people continue to do it. Psychologists decry the effects that social media is having on our children, but is it too late for them as well? Can our youth ignore their social needs to continually text their friends? Look around you the next time you are in a public place. Teens and young adults are fixated on their phone screens whether they are walking, eating, or even talking to companions.

So, you may ask, what is wrong with socialization, following the news, or a little entertainment? Nothing would be wrong if we spent only an hour or two a day doing it. But the average teen spends more than *seven* hours a day in front of a screen[7]. Between work and home, adults average *eleven* hours a day—almost all of our waking hours.[8] These hours of viewing, reading, texting, posting, and playing video games exact a price from your mental health. How fast can you point and click? Probably quite rapidly, so your screen probably changes rapidly and repeatedly. All that information, email, social posting, and gaming must be observed, mentally processed, and remembered somewhere. Your conscious brain is bearing the brunt of that overwhelming chore. Though it can be a lot of fun being constantly plugged into the internet universe, it may be pulling you down at the same time. How can that much time doing anything *not* affect your brain? What is the price of all that screen time? Is the content of all of that posting and communication uplifting and inspiring? Is it making you a better person?

This discussion will not be allowed to devolve into an attack on cell phones, the internet, or social media. Such an attack would be fruitless, because all three are here to stay. Given that fact, it is up to each individual to decide how much screen time is really necessary and how much becomes detrimental to your well-being.

Neuroplasticity

Neuroplasticity is a term used to describe the moldabilty or plasticity of our minds. Usually neuroplasticity is great. It allows our brains to adjust to new situations, such as a big move, going to college, getting married, and having children. It allows us to learn new languages and eventually speak them fluently, with no more thought than speaking your mother tongue.

But your brain will learn bad habits as quickly as it will learn good ones. For example, have you ever been addicted to a television series? Watching the first few episodes is so enjoyable that your brain starts to ingrain the characters and plot into pathways of thought. Watching a few more episodes further reinforces those pathways. If you don't watch the series for a few days, you actually start to miss the program as you might miss seeing a loved one. It can be a little scary as you start to obsess about a TV program. In any case, your brain moves very quickly to accommodate your new interests. Once a mental pathway is established and enjoyed, your brain will yearn to follow it over and over.

Thus, being on the internet, email, or social media for several hours a day *must* be changing the way you think. Your brain is usually fully engaged in such binge sessions. You are reading and thinking, and then liking, reacting, wording your responses, and posting them. If you are like many people, you do this over and over again, dozens of times a day and usually every day of the year. Such repetition *must* be etching deep ruts into your brain. Your brain learns that short texts, forming instant opinions, and then posting short (but often emotional) posts is how you want to communicate. After all, this is what you are doing every day, so your brain changes the way you think so you can be even better at attending to your email, social media, and other communications through the internet.

The effects of the internet are complex, and we will have further discussions about them. For now, we can note that many people, especially youth, are experiencing negative stresses due to their computers and cell phones, which are correlated with the occurrence of clinical depression.

Spiritual Depression

Another type of depression is affecting our younger generations, though you won't find as many articles about it in the latest magazines. Our culture is experiencing a widespread spiritual downturn, and all religions are feeling its effects. Fewer people believe in God, fewer pray regularly, and fewer still attend Church services. Research into this trend is generally done by surveying both our younger and older generations. Such an approach is common as a means to compare how our lives differ from those of our parents and grandparents. Though some of the date ranges may differ, here is a list of the latest four generations:

- Baby Boomers: born between 1946 and 1964
- Generation X: born between 1965 and 1980
- Millennials (or Generation Y): born between 1981 and 1996
- iGeneration (or Generation Z) born between 1997 and 2012

This latest generation was nicknamed the "iGeneration" because these young people have never known a world without the internet, iPhone, or iPad. The Millennial Generation (or the Y Generation) came of age during the rollover to a new millennium and the rise of social media. Cell phones, electronic tablets, laptops, Google, and social media have always been a part of their lives as well.

In 2018, Pew Research Center telephone surveys found that only 65 percent of American adults identified themselves as Christians. This percentage had dropped a full 12 percent over the past decade. Meanwhile, the religiously unaffiliated share of the population, consisting of people who identify themselves as atheistic, agnostic, or "nothing in particular," now stands at 26 percent, up from 17 percent in 2009.[9] A second independent study run by the General Social Survey found that in 2004, when the oldest Millennials were becoming twenty-something adults, 15 percent of the population responded that they never attended church. By 2018, 30 percent of those surveyed indicated that they never attended church.[10] These trends are worldwide. As of 2018, just over 33 percent of US adults attend church each week. However, church attendance in European countries averages 25 percent or less. Only 20 percent of our Canadian neighbors attend church each week.[11]

This is not really a surprise. It is well known that religious congregations have been graying for decades. In another Pew Research report titled "The Age Gap in Religion Around the World," we learn:

> Recent surveys have found that younger adults are far less likely than older generations to identify with a religion, believe in God or engage in a variety of religious practices. But this is not solely an American phenomenon: Lower religious observance among younger adults is common around the world, according to a new analysis of Pew Research Center surveys conducted in more than 100 countries and territories over the last decade.[12]

There is little doubt that, as a nation and as a world, we are not as religiously oriented as we have been in the past. These trends are very widespread, and we are seeing decreases in church activity throughout The Church of Jesus Christ of Latter-day Saints as well.

As just discussed, *mental* depression is affecting our younger generations more than our older generations. Likewise, *spiritual* depression is affecting the younger Millennials and Generation X more than the Baby Boomer and older generations. As noted in *The Next Mormons*,

Pew discovered that in 2007, 70 percent of respondents who had been in the LDS Church in childhood still self-identified as Mormons as adults, but in 2014 that figure had dipped to 64 percent. Among Millennials, the rate of retention was slightly lower still, at 62 percent. The GSS *(General Social Survey)* shows more dramatic losses among Mormons and confirms that much of this change is being driven by Generation Xers and Millennials.[13]

Once again, critics may make the argument that the traditional social and cultural norms of the Church are driving away young, progressive, politically aware younger generations. But those standards have existed for over 150 years. Though Millennials may think that their social consciousness exceeds that of all past generations, they lack historical perspective in that judgment. For centuries, younger generations have struggled against rules and standards—be they political, social, or religious—of their times. Over those hundreds of years, younger generations either abandoned these dictates or came to accept them. We are finding that many of the Generation Xers and Millennials are forsaking the spiritual and religious aspects of their lives in much greater numbers than past generations. Again, one must question, "Why?"

Without an answer to this question, churches and faithful parents are left struggling to understand why their young adults are leaving church and what they might do to stem the tide. Perhaps because of the relative isolation of the members of the Church in Utah, The Church of Jesus Christ of Latter-day Saints was able to delay the crises that other Christian religions have had to face for the past decade. But that delay is over. As explained by author Jana Riess,

> It's tempting to fixate on things the LDS church is or is not doing as the primary explanation for those membership losses, arguing that the church is alienating young people with its antigay rhetoric, its treatment of women, and its superannuated leadership. While this book presents statistical evidence that some of those reasons do factor into why more Millennials are leaving the LDS Church, a major explanation for disaffiliation is the changing religious landscape in America. Mormonism is not an island.[14]

The reasons behind this exodus of young people from religion are numerous and diverse. Each disaffiliated person will have different issues, frustrations, and disappointments with their spiritual journey. So, in our discussions, we will not try to list the reasons (or the counterarguments) for a young person who is disheartened with their faith.

Likewise, the reasons behind the increase in mental depression are numerous and diverse. Again, no one suffering from this malady will have the same issues, frustrations, and disappointments with their earthly journey as another. Likewise, we are not going to try to list the reasons (or the counterarguments) for mental depression. This is a book about your brain and your spirit and how they interact. If today's world is presenting challenges to our mind and spirit that we have not witnessed before, we should at least be aware of them.

This chapter presents the premise that we are subjecting our minds and spirits to the greatest abundance of information, opinions, news, hostility, and criticism we have ever seen. While being well informed is good, being besieged by marketers, bad news reports, and snarky social media followers *all day long* is unhealthy for your mind. What's more, you are opening the door to these influences every time you pull out your cell phone, tablet, or laptop. It would be impractical to suggest that you clear your life of all media. But you should try to understand what is going on in your brain and then make your own decisions as to your path forward.

How Do You Think?

Numerous books have been written about the effect the internet and social media have had on our society, especially on our children. There is no question that our media outlets provide more information on current events, global crises, and sales at the local mall than we have ever had before. There is so much content at our fingertips that we may not notice how its delivery is affecting us.

Neuroplasticity has already been defined as the ability of your brain to change itself so it can respond faster and more accurately to the activities you most value. The value you place on a specific activity is measured by how much time you spend on it. If you want to get better at playing a sport or musical instrument, you must practice, practice, practice. Your brain gets better at guiding your body to accomplish the perfect backswing or chord transition. So, if you spend hours a day responding to emails and texts, then your mind concludes that this activity must be very important you. Trying to help you excel in your new career path, your brain will forge new mental pathways to help you become a master emailer. This may mean overwriting neuron pathways that you aren't using much anymore—such as the focus required to read a novel or textbook. It is the price you pay for your choice. As a result of how you spend your time, your brain changes the way it thinks.

In his excellent book *The Shallows—What the Internet Is Doing to Our Brains*, author Nicholas Carr examines the effects the internet is having on our society. First, he looks at how the internet has affected him personally:

> I'm not thinking the way I used to think. I feel it most strongly when I'm reading. I used to find it easy to immerse myself in a book or a lengthy article. My mind would get caught up in the twists of the narrative or the turns of the argument, and I'd spend hours strolling through long stretches of prose. That's rarely the case anymore. Now my concentration starts to drift after a page or two. I get fidgety, lose my thread, begin looking for something else to do. ...media aren't just channels of information. They supply the stuff of thought, but they also shape the process of thought. And what the Net seems to be doing is chipping away my capacity for concentration and contemplation.[15]

The Edge is a website that asks experts in a field to reply to one major social question a year. In 2010, they asked, "How is the internet changing the way you think?" and then compiled the answers. Few questioned the fact that they were thinking differently; fewer still were happy with the results of those changes.[16]

Personally, it deeply bothers me that I might be losing the ability to delve into thoughtful reading and study. The fact that I am becoming more adept at checking social media or responding to texts does not comfort me. If we are to seek to "know the mysteries which are great and marvelous" (D&C 6:11), how can we do that if we can't concentrate on reading a book for more than a few minutes? To better understand how the internet may be affecting the spiritual side of our lives, perhaps a couple of examples of its effects on our gospel study are in order.

The Difference Between Scripture Study and Google

In Genesis 2:7, we are told that the Lord God breathed into Adam's nostrils and "man became a living soul." It is believed this event took place in about 4000 BC, so mankind has been seeking the meaning to that phrase for over six thousand years. Plato, Aristotle, and later Thomas Aquinas all wrote books about the soul. Students of religion have searched the scriptures and pored over writings by spiritual leaders to better understand their own soul and how it interacts through our bodies with the outside world. Men and women have dedicated much of their lives to answering such deep questions. Numerous scriptures encourage us to study and seek to understand. But the value in studying the scriptures is not to find all the answers so that we can stop studying. We derive profound value from the process of reading and contemplating what was read. Through this process we gain far deeper understandings and spiritual insights about our place on earth and why we are here. To study and understand our soul, its purpose, and its afterlife has been a worthy mission of dedicated students for centuries.

Now let's look at a more modern approach to studying this scripture. Googling the phrase "man became a living soul" provides about 99,700,000 results in 0.46 seconds. If you spent five seconds on each hit, it would take you over fifteen years to view them all. Granted, many of those hits will be repeats. But if you want to read millions of opinions about how "man became a living soul" and what those words mean, Google is certainly the place to go. Ironically, we tend to accept that millions of responses somehow make them authoritative. Could nearly 100 million answers be wrong? More important, the answers are right there in front of you. It didn't take years to compile them. It took less than half a second. If a generation grows up expecting every question to be answered in mere seconds, can that generation ever be patient enough to study and ponder their scriptures?

Flash Judgment

Not only is obtaining information from the internet blindingly fast, but so are the judgments we make and post about that news. Most social media sites offer the same general approach to their viewers. A news story (newspaper blogs), a photograph (Instagram), a personal experience (Facebook), or someone's comment (Twitter) is posted for you to view or read. You are then encouraged to like or dislike the post and, if you wish, to leave your own comments or opinion. You can then repost the story or photo for your followers, who can then make their own comments and share the string with other friends. It's an easy process, requiring only a few minutes to read the post, form an opinion, and write your judgment. Social media is based on being quick and easy.

However, quick and easy doesn't work to make sense of many news items. News from foreign countries must be put into the context of their society and culture. We can criticize conditions in Africa, the drug trade in South America, or the treatment of women in the Middle East. But do we understand these foreign people and their societies? Are we aware of the history and traditions that shaped their actions today? Do we understand the politics and environment of foreign lands and the pressures on its peoples? The same questions can be asked about historical figures. Many voices condemn the Founding Fathers for not banning slavery in the Constitution. Others denounce key historical figures for statements on minorities, women, or gays made decades ago. Historians unanimously and continuously encourage us to judge historical events only in the context of their time and place. What was the political and social environment of the time?

In social media, there is no time for such study. From our time and place of exceptional comfort and security, it is quite easy to become offended by the actions of strangers who lived in past centuries or in foreign lands. Social media provides a ready and easy outlet for expressing outrage. Very few responses ever consider the context of the time or place of the report, because jumping directly to condemnation is so much easier. Since most of us normally share our opinions with like-minded friends, hastily formed conclusions are usually affirmed and celebrated. Thus, the mentality of forming immediate opinions with no background checks has developed. In the past decade, many people have also become very critical of Latter-day Saint Church leaders from early Church history. In an open response to these accusations, the Church has commissioned its history department to write a new series of narrative history books. But one has to wonder why these severe judgments have become so popular.

History books always try to provide historical context—descriptions of the lifestyles, politics, customs, and even misconceptions of the time. Such background encourages readers to form fairer judgments of government and church leaders of bygone eras. But a 280-character tweet or any similar posting simply does not have time or space to establish a foundation upon which to build a fair, judicious opinion. Yet texts and posts are the way we choose to debate such topics today. We must ask ourselves, "As a society, are we losing the ability to consider context as we judge those who lived in other times and places?"

Flash judgment is unfair to those being judged, not only because context is not considered but because expectations can be set at unattainable heights. Our default setting is to expect that people act logically and morally at all times, especially if they are affiliated with religion. But such expectations rather deny the reality that *everyone* stumbles though life, doing their best, but making mistakes on a daily basis. Patrick Q. Mason wrote a well-considered response to such unfair expectations of early Church leaders in his book *Planted*. As he points out,

> Shouldn't the church, if it is really God's and really true, be somehow immune or at least elevated? Paradoxically, the scriptural answer to that question is a resounding "no." . . . Adam and Eve fall, Noah gets drunk, Abraham lies, Sarah is jealous, Jacob deceives, Joseph deceives, Moses murders, Joshua and Saul commit genocide, David commits adultery, Jonah runs from God, Elisha summons bears to kill forty-two children for calling him bald—and these are the good guys![17]

President Dieter F. Uchtdorf has offered his own observations about early Church leaders: "And, to be perfectly frank, there have been times when members or leaders in the Church have simply made mistakes. There may have been things said or done that were not in harmony with our values, principles, or doctrine. I suppose the Church would be perfect only if it were run by perfect beings."[18]

It is well known that studying the scriptures and learning other religious doctrine is a lifelong pursuit. Understanding comes with study, meditation, and prayer. It takes patience, as it may take years for full understanding. These traits are the opposite of what the internet and social media teach. Your social media friends expect your judgments immediately. Delays caused by meditation and deeper considerations are frowned upon. If you take a day or two to think something through, your followers will have probably moved on to discussions about the next press release in your absence.

In most ways, the Millennials and iGeneration are like all the previous generations before them. Like all new generations, they are demanding answers to age-old questions. But, because of the environment in which they were raised, these two generations have a different mentality about how to run their search. Having been raised with Google, many young adults do not understand that answers to the deeper questions of life are not immediate, complete, or politically correct. They don't seem to realize that putting those answers in context of their time and place is necessary before passing judgment on them. Answers to some questions in life are not immediate, simple, and cannot be prioritized on a Google results page.

For many young adults, the fact that they cannot immediately answer their mental and spiritual questions has become overwhelmingly disappointing. To them, it appears the spiritual side of their lives is not providing the answers to their personal quandaries regarding politics, morality, and their responsibilities toward God. Thus, many young people are dismissing spirituality and religion all together, walking away from church and God. This new mentality is disturbing as it affects our two latest generations and, almost certainly, will affect generations to follow.

A Reality Check

Has the internet really changed our brains and how we think? Are we as a people losing the ability to read long, thoughtful books and formulate fair responses to current events? Has your brain lost its desire to contemplate the wonders that books can teach you about your place in the universe? Possibly, but the internet and social media are not going away due to the concerns about their effects on our brains. Whatever the cause of your mental and spiritual unrest, you should endeavor to better care for the state of your mind. In Church services we discuss at length what we should do to sustain our spiritual health. But spiritual health rests on a foundation of our mental stability or, if you will, brain health. So, we should devote some time to understanding our brains and how they interact with our spirits.

In the past few decades, research on the brain has greatly advanced our understanding of our most complex organ. But there are still many mysteries as to how it functions. As one brain scientist lamented, "In truth, if we ever fully understand how the human brain knew how to pick up a glass of water, it would represent a major achievement."[19] After reviewing the brain, can we answer the question of how our brains interact with our spirits? Unfortunately, brain and spirit interaction has not been a topic of much research. But we do have some information on the topic that we can consider.

Rest assured that we are *not* going to conduct a highly technical review of brain chemistry and psychology. To understand your mind, you need to know a little about its basic mechanism and how it is affected by outside influences. Your brain is a highly complex tool. To comprehend how your conscious mind engages with your spiritual self, we need to start with a simple primer on the brain.

ENDNOTES

1. World Health Organization (WHO), who.int/mental_health/management/depression/wfmh_paper_depression_wmhd_2012.pdf, 6.
2. Diane McIntosh, *This Is Depression* (Vancouver: Page Two Books, 2019), 23.
3. Alex Korb, *The Upward Spiral* (Oakland, CA: New Harbinger Publications, 2015), 3.
4. Keith Kramlinger, M.D. editor, *Mayo Clinic on Depression* (Philadelphia, Mason Crest Publishers, 2001), 39.
5. verywellmind.com/who-discovered-depression-1066770
6. Kristen Rogers, CNN Health (Oct. 29, 2019), "US teens use screens more than seven hours a day on average—and that's not including school work," cnn.com/2019/10/29/health/common-sense-kids-media-use-report-wellness/index.html.
7. Scripps.org,"How Much Screen Time Is Too Much?" (Feb. 22, 2019), scripps.org/news_items/6626–how-much-screen-time-is-too-much.
8. samhsa.gov/data/sites/default/files/cbhsq-reports/NSDUHNationalFindingsReport2018/NSDUHNationalFindingsReport2018.pdf, 41–42.
9. pewforum.org/2019/10/17/in-u-s-decline-of-christianity-continues-at-rapid-pace/
10. gssdataexplorer.norc.org/trends/Religion%20&%20Spirituality?measure=attend
11. pewforum.org/2018/06/13/how-religious-commitment-varies-by-country-among-people-of-all-ages/
12. pewforum.org/2018/06/13/the-age-gap-in-religion-around-the-world/
13. Jana Riess, *The Next Mormons,* (New York: Oxford University Press, 2019) 4–5.
14. Riess, *The Next Mormons,* 6.
15. Nicholas Carr, *The Shallows—What the Internet is doing to our Brains,* (New York: W.W. Norton & Company, 2010), 5–6.
16. edge.org/annual-question/how-is-the-internet-changing-the-way-you-think
17. Patrick Q. Mason, *Planted* (Salt Lake City: Deseret Book, 2015), 51–52.
18. Dieter F. Uchtdorf, "Come Join with Us," *Ensign*, November 2013, 22.
19. John Medina, *Brain Rules* (Seattle, WA: Pear Press, 2014), 4.

CHAPTER 2

The Brain

The brain is a very important and delicate organ—so your body has been specifically designed to protect it. Your skull is a hard, protective bone that forms a natural helmet around your brain. Under that bone is a thick, fibrous membrane encasing the brain called the dura mater, which is Latin for "tough mother." As its name implies, this membrane surrounds the brain like an overly protective mother, providing a secondary defense to blows to the skull. Finally, our brains float in a semi-viscous cerebrospinal fluid that further helps to cushion the brain from impact damage. In the design of your body, protection of the brain was apparently of central importance. Your body dedicates a large amount of its resources to the brain. Though it only constitutes 2 percent of your body mass, it consumes 20 percent of the total calories your body uses.[1] The brain is so highly complex that centuries of study by very intelligent researchers have yet to reveal all its secrets.

The thought of studying your brain chemistry may be a little intimidating. Though we will briefly consider the actions of neurons, please know that we are not going to get too detailed in our discussion. But to understand depression—be it mental, spiritual, or both—we must start with the brain. When your car breaks down, you take it into the repair shop, not knowing or even caring what needs to be done to fix it. You know it is the job of the mechanic to fix your automobile without your help. However, when your brain has a problem, only you can fix it. Therapists can give counsel from the sidelines, but it is you who must adjust your thinking and behaviors. So, unlike your car, you need a basic understanding of how your mind works to best maintain it.

As those who suffer from it will attest, depression acts like a silent enemy that can attack at seemingly random times. It can magnify simple inconveniences into major stumbling blocks. We have pharmaceutical and counseling weapons at our disposal to fight this war, which we will consider later. But to start this discussion, you have to understand the combatants—your mind and the severe despondency that can affect it. Sun Tzu, a Chinese general, wrote *The Art of War* in about 500 BC. In it, he gives this recommendation for winning such a war: "If you know the *enemy* and know *yourself,* you need not fear the result of a hundred battles. If you know yourself but not the enemy, for every victory gained you will also suffer a defeat. If you know neither the enemy nor yourself, you will succumb in every battle."[2]

When it comes to the battle between your mind and depression, you don't want to be the unprepared bystander totally confused and bewildered by your mood changes, frustration, and bouts of exhaustion. Sun Tzu was correct. If you come to know an enemy well enough to recognize its tactics, you can immediately establish your defenses and repulse its attacks. But, as Sun Tzu declares, you must also know *yourself* to establish your best defense. Since it is your mind that is under attack, you must understand your mind, which will be our mission in the next pages. You won't need to become a brain surgeon, but you must be willing to do some introspection. You don't need to memorize the Latin names for parts of the brain, but you should know how your brain responds to the different stimuli, be they chemical or sensorial. The next few paragraphs are somewhat technical. But to understand your brain, how it functions, and how drugs affect it, there must be an introduction to neurons.

From outward appearances, your brain is a three-pound lump of gray matter that sits inside your skull. However, your brain is actually a network of about 100 billion neurons with about 100 trillion connecting points, or synapses.[3] Each neuron looks like a normal cell with a nucleus, but with branches and a long tail. These branches that come off of the cell body are called dendrites, and they extend out from the cell to collect signals from surrounding neurons. The long tail, or axon, can be lengths less than a millimeter in your brain to a meter long from your feet to your brain. The axon terminal branches broadcast signals out to the dendrites of the next neurons that need to receive the signal.

When a neuron receives a signal from its dendrites that must be passed on to other neurons, a mini-pulse of electricity is generated and sent down the tail, or axon, to a number of axon terminals at its very end. One neuron can have hundreds of axon terminals, all of which are affected by the traveling pulse. When the signal arrives at each axon terminal, it must be transmitted to the dendrites of the next neuron. To do that, the signal needs to make it across the synapse, a small space between the axon terminal of the transmitting neuron to the dendrite of the receiving neuron. To do this, the signal must be converted from an electrical pulse to a chemical signal. When prompted by a large enough pulse, the axon terminal releases chemical neurotransmitters into the synapse. The neurotransmitters float across the gap and bond to receptors on the dendrites of the receiving neuron. This bonding stimulates the receiving neuron to generate its own electrical pulse which is sent down its axon. The process may continue over thousands of neurons—but it is, of course, very fast. If you touch a sharp object with your index finger, the time it takes you to respond, called latency, is generally less than a tenth of a second.

Mapping the Brain

In the earliest days of researching the brain, surgeons relied on head injuries for much of their data. Industrial accidents and battlefield injuries often result in punctured skulls and injuries to the brain. Doctors correlated the part of the brain that was damaged with the resulting disabilities of the victim. This allowed doctors to start figuring out how different parts of the brain affected behavior. The most famous head injury in the history of brain research occurred in 1848 when a man named Phineas Gage was setting explosives for railroad construction. A charge exploded prematurely, and Phineas ended up with a metal rod protruding from his head. Miraculously, despite the massive brain injury, Phineas survived. Though he appeared fully functional, friends and work associates reported a major personality change in him. Before the incident, Phineas had had a pleasant, easygoing nature. After the accident he became impatient and irritable. When part of your brain becomes dysfunctional, memories, senses, and even personality can be affected.

More information came to light through autopsies. In 1860, Dr. Pierre Paul Broca diagnosed a patient named Leborgne with a severe language deficit. Leborgne could understand what people told him and could follow their instructions. But when he tried to speak, this handicapped man could only create unintelligible mumblings. When Leborgne died, Dr. Broca examined his brain in an autopsy. He found a region in the front part of the left hemisphere that had been shriveled due to syphilis or other disease. In the course of his career, Broca found eight other people with the same disability and the same damaged part of the brain. Now called Broca's area, we know that that this small area of the brain is where we put our words together in creating speech.

In 1875, Dr. Carl Wernicke treated a patient who could speak but had lost his ability to understand his own language. He could not follow even the simplest instruction. When the patient died, Dr. Wernicke found a completely separate area of the brain further back from Broca's area that was damaged. Now called Wernicke's area, we now know this part of the brain is used in language comprehension.[4]

In the early 1900s, Dr. Wilder Penfield of Canada developed a practice of finding and removing scar tissue in the brain that caused epileptic seizures.[5] To find such scar tissue, Dr. Penfield opened up the brain and stimulated different areas with an electric probe. One of the great ironies of our bodies is that the brain—the operations center of our nervous system—has no pain receptors of its own. Thus, Dr. Penfield's patients could be awake during their brain surgery and tell him what they felt when different areas of their brains were stimulated. Did shocking this part of the brain cause the patient to think he was hearing things or cause a muscular twitch in the leg? Did stimulating another part of the brain cause the patient to think he was tasting a strange food or evoke a memory from childhood? By correlating the point of the brain being stimulated with the response of patients, a map of the brain was gradually created.

In this past century, brain imaging has been developed that can look at blood flow in the brain. It has been discovered that your brain will send more blood into the areas of the brain needing it most. So, if you are listening to "Beethoven's 5th Symphony," a functional magnetic resonance image will show that your audio cortex is receiving more blood flow to better listen to and appreciate the music. Such imaging was used to fill in the brain maps and chart where more specific bodily functions reside in the brain. Maps of the brain, superimposed on a replica of a brain or skull, are readily available for purchase.

Brain Disorders

Before 1900, the medical community understood very little about mental disorders. The brain was just too complex. For no apparent reason, some children were born with mental retardation, neurological dysfunction, or extreme behavioral issues. Some people developed problems after a severe illness, head injury, or traumatic event. But issues inside the brain were simply too complex for physicians of the time to treat or heal. Most people thought that issues of the mind were caused by possession by evil spirits, curses, or punishments by God. In 1790, a French physician named Philippe Pinel founded the medical practice of psychiatry. Dr. Pinel was the first authoritative figure to proclaim that psychiatric issues were a result of disease and not moral character. He even recognized that many mental disorders were a result of heredity, while others were caused by traumas from which the victim could not fully recover.

Due to the slow accumulation of knowledge, for many years psychiatric disorders such as schizophrenia, depression, bipolar disorder, and anxiety were considered simple behavioral problems. These diseases did not leave evidence of physical damage to the brain, so bizarre behavior was considered to be under voluntary control. These psychiatric disabilities were judged to be due to either a poor upbringing, simple lack of self-control, or of a weak spirit that could not control its own body. "Until about 1800, only disorders that resulted from visible damage to the brain, as seen at autopsy, were considered medical disorders. . . . Disorders of thought, feeling, and mood, as well as drug addiction, did not appear to be associated with detectable brain damage and, as a result, were considered to be defects in a person's moral character."[6]

But the learning continued. In the early 1900s, Franz Kallmann documented that psychiatric disorders such as schizophrenia and bipolar disorder follow family lines and are often hereditary in nature. This proved that mental illness could be passed from one generation to the next. Characteristics of each disorder were identified and documented so the disease could be named. Years later, DNA sequencing determined which genomes were responsible for each issue.[7]

We have always understood that, when someone has a physical disability, their handicap is due to the fact that their body is a damaged. The damage may have been genetic, caused by a problem that occurred in the womb, or due to a childhood accident. There is never a suspicion of a character flaw or lack of self-discipline, as has been true in the history of mental disease. As a society, we have learned to not judge mental disabilities or retardation as evidence of an evil within the handicapped person's spirit. For over two hundred years psychiatry has recognized that mental disorders are *not* indicators of a weak soul or mind.

However, a stigma that poor mental health is a weakness in character still exists today. For example, while many people will confidently tell friends and coworkers that they are taking anti-inflammatories to treat their body aches, they are often more hesitant to reveal that they are taking antidepressants for ongoing despondency. For such individuals, taking antidepressants seems to admit to the world that they are too weak to handle the stresses of life without some pharmaceutical help. Did any of our ancestors suffer from depression and anxiety? Absolutely they did. But there were simply no treatments for them to consider. Depression is one of the fastest growing diseases in the world today, but fortunately pharmaceutical help is available. Treatments exist and ignoring them only adds to your exhaustion and despondency.

The Subconscious Mind

The fact that we walk, breathe, hiccup, and laugh without thinking about it has been recognized for centuries. Hippocrates (460–377 BC), Thomas Aquinas (1225–1274), Rene Descartes (1596—1650), and others proposed and developed the concept of a subconscious mind. Indeed, we do many activities without planning or thought. In 1920, Sigmund Freud taught that many of man's aberrant behaviors and psychological disorders were due to problems that were well beneath our level of consciousness.[8] By the mid-1900s, as researchers uncovered the full breadth of subconscious activity of the brain, they realized that we don't really know ourselves very well. Our subconscious mind regulates how quickly we get angry or jealous, though the conscious mind can step in and modify our emotions. What we see as beautiful or sexually attractive is determined by our subconscious mind. The majority of our personality is found in our subconscious mind.

People have always been fascinated by the fact that we have a subconscious mind, essentially another self, hidden in the recesses of our brains. There have been many attempts to tap into that part of our minds— hypnosis, deep mediation techniques, and dream interpretation to name a few. Having a subconscious mind is a little scary. Should we be held responsible for what we say aloud as we dream? If a man sleepwalks and commits a crime, should he be arrested and jailed for his actions?

Studies of the subconscious mind have generated more questions than answers. We have learned that the subconscious is an under-appreciated control center of your body. Without you ever having to think about it, all your bodily processes are monitored and controlled. Through nerve, hormone, and other messenger systems, the subconscious brain controls your heart, lungs, and digestion. You shiver when you are cold and sweat when you are hot. Your physical reactions to fear, sexual arousal, physical exertion, dreams, and even surprise are all controlled by your subconscious mind. When you walk, do you have to consciously command each muscle to contract at the proper time? Do you consciously adjust your stride when your inner ear indicates you are slightly off balance?

Interestingly, most of our subconscious actions and responses come preprogrammed in our DNA. For example, I have never eaten rancid meat. There is no experience in my memory of ever eating rotten meat, causing me severe food poisoning and a night of regurgitating everything in my stomach. So why does the odor of putrefied meat cause me to retch, unconsciously cover my nose, and quickly turn away? My brain has a preprogrammed response to rotted meat or other spoiled foods which I have had since birth. No matter how hungry I am, my preprogrammed response to the smell (and taste) of putrefied meat will fight against any desire to eat it. My brain comes preprogrammed by my DNA to avoid rotten food that would certainly sicken and possibly kill me.

Other mental responses to smells and taste are programmed later in life. For example, when I was about ten years old, I came down with a bad case of the stomach flu. My father kindly brought me home a vanilla shake to help me feel better. I gobbled it down, of course, and immediately threw it up. My brain learned a lesson from that one experience—vanilla was dangerous. I could not stand the smell or taste of vanilla for many years to come. Eventually, that memory faded and I can safely drink a vanilla shake now. But my repugnance to rotten meat is indelible and appears it will never fade.

Physical abilities that we first develop in our conscious mind can be moved into our subconscious mind. Consider learning to ride a bicycle. First, you must be extremely focused to keep the bike balanced, the handle bars steady, and the pedals moving. Your cerebral cortex is very involved in learning the ability. But after you have learned the skill, it moves into your subconscious. You don't have to think about riding your bike anymore. You can talk to companions and admire the view as you bike along. The same goes for learning to tie your shoes or buttoning your shirt.

In golf, players are encouraged to practice their swing until they have developed "muscle memory." In reality, muscles don't have a memory, but your subconscious mind does. Once a movement is fully worked into your subconscious, you can accomplish that act without thinking about it. You can drive your car while talking on your cell phone because you give control over the driving to your subconscious. However, please note that your subconscious mind is not as good a driver as your conscious mind, which explains why talking on your cell phone while driving is illegal in many states. Otherwise, moving chores to your subconscious mind is the ultimate step in multitasking.

We rarely think about our unconscious minds, but it is hard to over-state the extent to which you use it. Do you consciously think before laughing at a funny comment made by a friend? Do you think about your facial expressions before making them? As one author concluded, "The unexpected part of the news is that the conscious *you* is the smallest bit-player in the brain."[8] It soon becomes obvious that your unconscious mind makes up a great deal of your personality. As stated by philosophy professor Patricia S. Churchland, "Surprisingly, perhaps, even your spontaneity relies pretty heavily on your unconscious brain, as you talk, laugh, gesture, and so forth. So the *real* you, the *you* of Saturday morning at home, is deeply integrated with your unconscious activities."[9]

Having such an active, completely unconscious side of our brain has implications regarding the spiritual side of our bodies and will be discussed further in the chapter on our consciousness and soul.

Your Senses

Whether you are walking down the sidewalk or reading a book, your brain is sorting out sensory communications from all parts of your body. In reality, your brain is in a very quiet, perfectly dark chamber within your skull. But through your senses, your brain is apprised of what is going on outside. Vision is the most dominant sense—about a third of your brain is dedicated to processing the input from your eyes.[10] But your ears, nose, mouth, and skin are all sending continuous messaging as well. Your brain is processing all of these signals. If your conscious mind had to sort through each visual image and smell or the varying pressures on your feet as you walk, it would be overloaded. It couldn't keep up. So most of these signals are processed by the unconscious brain, which is actually much faster at it than your conscious brain. The only time your conscious brain needs to be brought online is if something is different. Think about the last time you walked into your own house. Your eyes probably quickly swept through the family room and kitchen. Did you register and check off each piece of furniture in the room? Or did your eyes stop at, say, only the puddle of spilled milk in front the refrigerator? Your unconscious mind detected that milk on your floor is not within the normal image you have of your kitchen, so it made your conscious mind aware of the discrepancy. Your conscious mind then took over and went into clean-up mode or upset-parent mode, whichever you chose.

The same process occurs as you walk down the street. Signals from the nerves on your feet tell your unconscious brain that all is going as expected. Nothing of interest is going on down here. Your inner ear confirms the fact that you are balanced, upright, and moving down the road. Your conscious mind wanders, thinking about the state of the world economy or your plans for the weekend. Then you step into an unseen pothole. The nerves in your feet are not feeling the pavement where it should be. Alarm bells are sent to your conscious brain that all is not well with your feet anymore. Your eyes quickly swing down to see what's going on. After sending this courtesy message to your conscious mind, your unconscious brain sends a message to the feet to lunge forward to get your legs under you again. Your arms unconsciously rise in front of you to protect yourself in the event of a full-fledged fall. You stumble a bit but manage to recover. You grumble about the roads and continue your walk, not even aware that the explosion of back and forth communications between your conscious mind and your unconscious brain just saved you from a face plant. As stated by David Eagleman in his book *The Brain*,

> It seems to require very little effort to recognize a friend's face, drive a car, get a joke, or decide what to grab from the refrigerator—but in fact these things are possible only because of the vast computations happening below your conscious awareness. Simple acts are underpinned by a massive labor force of neurons... You remain blissfully unaware of all their activity, but your life is shaped and colored by what's happening under the hood: how you act, what matters to you, your reactions, your loves and desires, what you believe to be true and false.[11]

So your brain, both conscious and unconscious, is constantly monitoring all the signals it is receiving from your eyes, ears, nose, mouth, skin, and inner ear to advise you of what is going on around you. The systems in your brain that monitor sensory input all run independently and continually.[12]

Memories

The next time you walk down the same street where you stumbled so badly, your brain may recognize that this was the stretch of road where you stepped into a pothole. You visually examine the road more carefully this time to be sure to avoid the hole. One of the main purposes of memory is to help remind us of danger and how to avoid it. But memories also remind us of good experiences, like the great lasagna we had at that little Italian restaurant downtown.

Like our senses, we access memories with a combination of our conscious mind and another subconscious part of our mind. Obviously, your memories cannot be kept active in your conscious mind. Such an overload of data would slow your conscious mind to a crawl, like a computer with a full hard drive. Memories are instead stored in a part of your mind that is accessible to your conscious mind, but that generally remains well below your normal level of consciousness. Sigmund Freud referred to this as the "preconscious mind."[13] There has been a great deal of work done in memory research. We have learned that memories are stored under different keywords or images. Thus you can look at a stretch of road and remember the pothole. Or you can notice another pothole in another city miles away and remember the pothole on the stretch of road where you almost face-planted. You can see the Italian place downtown and remember their great lasagna, or you can see a photo of a plate of lasagna and have a strong urge to drive downtown to have dinner.

With all of these potential triggers, the conscious mind is constantly bringing memories out of storage. If you see a cat, you may remember the orange tabby that you owned as a child. A song on the radio may trigger a memory of an experience you haven't thought about for years. A stranger at an airport with a prominent nose may remind you of someone else you knew decades ago. Smells are especially effective at bringing forth strong memories of experiences you had in another place and another time. So, not only is your brain processing all your visual images, smells, and nerve responses to touch, but it is also searching for memories that you might need or want to better understand those external stimuli. All of this is done to allow you to make good decisions.

Emotions

Emotions are kept in an unconscious part of your mind as well. Normally you will not consciously choose to get angry at something. Do you choose to be embarrassed? Do you choose to be afraid of the dark or things that go bump in the night? Normally each of these emotions occurs so quickly that your conscious mind is still figuring things out even as the emotion is well under way. Anger management courses teach participants to more quickly engage their conscious minds in harnessing emotional outbursts.

Strong emotions elicit life-saving responses from your body and brain. I was driving on an interstate in Phoenix one day with my wife and some friends. As we approached an overpass, I saw a car fly off the bridge above us, on a trajectory to land right on top of my car. Our lives were in danger and my emotions and subconscious mind took over. In a fraction of a second, my brain sent an urgent message to my adrenal glands, which shot a large dose of adrenaline into my bloodstream. Adrenaline is quite a drug, by the way. Everything around me suddenly went into slow motion. I watched the airborne car gradually turn upside down as it plummeted toward the pavement and us. I cranked my steering wheel, slammed on the breaks, and checked my rearview mirror, all before the free-falling car crashed on the road in front of us. Within a few seconds, the world returned to its normal pace. My buddy jumped out of the back seat to help, and I pulled the car to the curb. We assisted the accident victims until the police arrived.

Fear, excitement, and alarm all combined to stimulate my brain to think and react faster. My brain realized that I had to move quickly to avoid a serious accident. My adrenal glands pumped adrenaline into my bloodstream, and I went into hyperdrive for a few moments. I am grateful for that, as it possibly saved our lives. People often talk about "fighting their emotions" or trying to "take emotion out of the equation." This is the goal behind anger management and other destructive emotions. But emotions are extremely important in decision making. Too often we think of emotions as clouding our judgment, when we should be welcoming our emotions to help us make good decisions.

Perhaps an example is in order. If we just had logical minds, our society would be quite different than it is today. Logically, it is our responsibility to live out and enjoy our lives, contribute to society, and then pass on our places on earth to the next generation. Logically, those who contribute to the good of society are valued for their efforts. But what about those who are *not* contributing to society? What about the elderly in the nursing homes, living out the last years of their lives? What about the prisoners in our penitentiaries and jails? What about the severely mentally retarded and physically handicapped people living out their lives in care centers? Logically, these people are not only failing to contribute to society, but they have become a significant burden upon it. Emotionally, we feel sorry for these individuals and their situations. Logically however, given the premise of each generation's responsibility (prepare yourself), these people should be killed. Logically, why invest in people who cannot give back to society? But the emotional/spiritual side of each one of us recoils at the thought of such violence. In this case, compassion overrules logic. With all due respect to Mr. Spock and the Vulcans, a person or a society cannot be run on logic alone. On the other hand, society or an individual cannot base their lives on pure emotion either. Some of the worst decisions in a person's life are made at the height of emotion. One moment of passion brings an unwanted baby into the world. One moment of anger can result in the death of one person and lifelong imprisonment for another.

If your rational brain and emotional mind are in conflict, then the choice of which to follow can be difficult. But choices must be made, and we make them every day. The really hard questions are those that don't have an obvious logical or emotional winner. As one writer expressed it, "Because both of the neural systems battle to control the single output channel of behavior, emotions can tip the balance of decision making. This ancient battle has turned into a directive of sorts for many people: If it feels bad, it is probably wrong. There are many counter examples to this . . . , but emotion nonetheless serves as a generally useful steering mechanism for decision making."[14]

Your emotions reside in the limbic system of your brain, central to which is your amygdala. Your emotions are so important that they have their very own memory section, separate from your normal memory. When an intense emotion accompanies an event in your life, then your memory of the event becomes more intense. My wife has a normal rational brain memory, occasionally having problems remembering her multiplication tables. But her emotional brain memory is extraordinary. She remembers who gave her a favorite blouse and which Christmas she received it. She remembers family gatherings in intricate detail. Sadly, she also remembers what was said in our earliest marital disputes, a superpower which seems rather unfair to me.

Sorting Out the Voices in Your Head

In any decision, a multitude of voices in the form of thoughts, emotions, and ideas come from different areas of your brain. One has to wonder how that is possible. Since you only have one brain, how can it be possible for you to not be able to make up your mind? Or how can you ever be "of two minds" on a subject? How can you possibly argue with yourself? I realize the term "hearing voices in your head" usually refers to someone who is losing their grip on reality. But everyone has thoughts, memories, and emotions being brought to their conscious mind every waking minute of the day. If there was only one voice, multiple options to solve a problem would not even occur to you. On one hand, all your decisions would become very easy. On the other hand, such a simple-minded approach would also threaten your survival. Multiple thoughts *need* to occur to you. You should listen to the voice that warns you to look both ways before crossing the street and ignore the voice urging you to hurry carelessly along.

As an example, if it is a nice day outside, you may think about how nice it might be to go on a walk. One part of your mind may recall the memory that you got chilled on your last walk and it could happen again. The part of your brain monitoring your nervous system may remind you that you are still recovering from a pulled muscle in your calf—and it hurts a little more even as you think about it. The more self-disciplined part of your brain may remind you that some exercise would be very good for you. Another part of your brain may argue how nice it would be to feel the sun on your face and breathe some fresh air. You may remember your New Year's resolution to get outside more. If you think about your normal decision process, you will realize that different thoughts, memories, and emotions present their arguments. Of those five different voices that presented arguments in this example, which is *your* voice? One of the newest revelations about the brain is that they are *all* your voice. Your mind weighs the options presented by different parts of your mind and you make a decision. You either go on a walk or you don't.

One brain researcher calls this model the "team-of-rivals" framework of the brain.[15] There is no single voice when making a decision; your brain makes decisions by its mental committee. This new paradigm is important for our following discussions. In making a simple decision like, "Should I go to bed now?" different parts of your mind will submit their opinions. The memories storage may submit the fact that you have an early morning meeting and need to get a good night's sleep. Your emotions section may submit that you are still too wound up from the day to go to bed yet. The physical monitoring part of your brain will assess how tired your body feels at the moment of decision. The mental committee then argues the question for a few moments and makes a decision.

For really big decisions in your life, you can expect even more voices chiming in with recommendations. Should you buy the house you have been looking at? Should you quit your job and look for a new one? Should you marry your sweetheart? Is it the right time to start a family? Complex decisions will stimulate numerous arguments from all parts of your mind, so it takes more time for the mental committee to come to a decision. In moments of indecision, you may solicit the opinions of your friends and family. Logic, fear, love, frustration, and a host of other emotions will all contribute their arguments to the debate. Your conscious brain will look for correlation between your present dilemma and similar decisions you made in the past. Through it all, your mind knows it must make a decision. But the bigger the potential life change, the longer the committee will take to make it. The inner voices arguing about the best way forward can nearly drive you crazy.

So Who Are You Anyway?

Who are you? You are a composite of a number of ingredients, which we can address in chronological order. First, your mind and body are the construction of bone, cartilage, muscle, and brain tissue that were created and maintained by your DNA. This DNA was provided by your parents, so any blame or credit for the person you are is shared with them. If there were flaws in the DNA transcription leading to a physical or mental handicap, then that error has become a part of who you are in this life. Your DNA established if you are attractive, athletic, smart, talented at dance, or musically gifted. Thus, what your DNA created plays a significant role in defining your personality and will certainly have its effect on the spirit that inhabits that body.

Upon the physical foundation of your mind and body, we now add how you were nurtured as a child. How happy was your home life? Who were your peers? What were your successes and failures? The experiences you had during the developmental years of your childhood also determine much of the person you are today. Your childhood experiences will greatly depend upon your parents and other family members. Finally

The Brain

let's add in the experiences that you have chosen for yourself since you became an adult. Did you go to college? Do you believe in God and do you attend church regularly? Did you marry and has your marriage been a good experience? Have you had children and have they been a good experience for you?

Ironically, not even you are aware of many of the aspects of who you are, because they are stored in your unconscious mind. As one researcher and author explained it,

> When I talk to nonscientists about my work, they tend to wonder which is the "real" them, their conscious or their unconscious self. Some people think that the conscious self is the true self, because it reflects a person's intentions and what he is aware of doing. Others think that the unconscious self is the real self because it reflects what the person really believes down deep, not just the version of themselves that they want to present to the world. But the real answer is "both." We need to expand our idea of who is the "I."[16]

In the end, you are unique. You are the only person in the world with the DNA-determined structure of your brain, the memories of your childhood, your experiences, and the beliefs you hold dear. Your conscious and unconscious minds should be extremely important to you, because they *are* you. They determine the decisions you make today and thus shape your future. Your mind will decide if you are going to obey the commandments of God. Wherever "you" want to go in life, your mind is there to assist you. Hopefully, you are comfortable with that.

ENDNOTES

1. John Bargh, *Before You Know It* (New York City: Touchstone, 2017), 8.
2. (Sun Tzu, *The Art of War*; italics added.
3. Max Bertolero and Danielle S. Bassett, "How Matter Becomes Mind," *Scientific American*, July 2019, Vol. 321 #1, 28.
4. Eric R. Kandel, *The Disordered Mind* (New York: Farrar, Straus and Giroux, 2018) 11.
5. Kandel, *The Disordered Mind*, 13.
6. Ibid., 9, 22.
7. Stanislas Dehaene, *Consciousness and the Brain* (New York City: Penguin Books, 2014), 50–52.
8. David Eagleman, *Incognito* (New York: Vintage Books), 99.
9. Patricia S. Churchland, *Touching a Nerve* (New York: W.W. Norton & Company, 2013), 208.

10. Eagleman, *Incognito,* 205.
11. David Eagleman, *The Brain* (New York: Pantheon Books, 2015), 68.
12. Michael S. Gazzaniga, *The Consciousness Instinct* (New York City: Farrar, Straus, & Giroux, 2018), 115.
13. Gazzaniga, *The Consciousness Instinct*, 51.
14. Eagleman, *Incognito,* 114.
15. Eagleman, *Incognito,* 101.
16. Bargh, *Before You Know It*, 17.

CHAPTER 3

The Holy Ghost: One Voice among Many

There is an important reason to understand this new paradigm that your brain contains numerous voices. Through all this internal debate going on in their heads, faithful followers of God will often seek His counsel in prayer. His is the inner voice of the Spirit that you really want to hear. If God would just make His opinion known through a spiritual manifestation, then the decision is made! Whether you believe that voice is your own spirit, the Holy Ghost, or the Holy Ghost communicating with your spirit, you should always remember that the voice of the Spirit is just one voice among many. The hardest part of prayers pleading for guidance is to figure out *if* the Spirit is casting a vote and, if so, which voice it is.

There are, of course, hundreds of books written about prayer and how to discern God's will. Such books will generally suggest that you have faith, obey the commandments, pray, and be patient. This is simple and good advice, of course. But for many people the spiritual answer is not forthcoming. Often, a deadline is approaching and a decision must be made. It can be very frustrating.

Why We Are on Earth

While I was on a mission in Mexico, I taught that we had to come to earth as part of the eternal plan of happiness. I explained to investigators of the Church that we came here to have the opportunity to have a body, to develop faith, and to make good, righteous choices. Since my mission, I have modified my understanding of these three aspects of earth life. First, I discovered that learning to control a body was relatively easy. We learn to walk within a couple of years after birth, we are talking within a couple more, and we are fairly accomplished at controlling our bodies by the time we are, say, five years old. However, learning to use and control our minds takes a lifetime. So, yes, you came to earth to receive a body, but your body could be considered just a vehicle for your mind. It is mainly your mind that your spirit came to earth to receive. You learn *with* your mind and *from* your mind at the same time.

We are here on earth to learn to have faith. Once again, your brain plays the starring role in this process. Your testimony is a result of your choices. When you feel the witness of the Holy Ghost, you have a number of choices. Your brain can choose to ignore those promptings, brushing them off simply as emotional yearnings of your heart. Your brain can choose to recognize the promptings as confirmations that what you are reading, hearing, or saying is true. As it does so, your brain accepts that these messages are of God—and thus you develop a testimony.

There is one last decision your brain must make in this process of developing a testimony. As a result of your spiritual witnesses, do you attend church, pray, and accept church callings? I have known a number of inactive Saints who had strong testimonies of the truthfulness of the gospel. But due to an offense taken or an agonizing life experience, these Church members decided that their lives would be easier if they stopped attending church. Members have different responses to spiritual conversion. A testimony of the gospel does not always predicate a lifetime of prayer or religious observance. The brain must decide, and different brains will arrive at different decisions.

There are other complexities of the mind and spirit interface. When lessons about decisions are given in Sunday School class, it often sounds like there only two choices—the righteous one and the unrighteous one. But when you must make a decision, rarely is it a simple decision between right and wrong or righteous and unrighteous. That would be like walking into an ice cream shop and having a choice of two flavors, say, liver-flavored (wrong) and chocolate (right). That decision would be pretty easy, unless you are one of the ten people on earth who really likes liver. Most ice cream shops have dozens of options from which to choose. Few of them would be considered wrong or unrighteous. As was discussed in the last chapter, to teach you this skill, your brain automatically comes up with multiple responses to any given question. How better to teach you to make good decisions than to provide you with multiple options for any given question and make you choose the best response? The more important decisions in life will have dozens of options—and your brain is programmed to present as many to your conscious mind as it can find. We should not look at this ability as a frustrating problem. It is an opportunity to make the best decision we can and then learn from it.

So, though we are on the earth to learn to make good choices, many people look at their life decisions with the single-minded purpose to discover the one their Heavenly Father wants them to choose. Hundreds of books have been written about how to get answers from God. Few of them mention that the Lord will probably be willing to only answer a few of your life's most important questions, because if God always pointed out the way for you, then what would you learn? You were sent to earth to learn how to use your brain to make good decisions—not to get all the answers from the Master.

One last point needs to be made here. Making bad decisions is a key learning experience in life—much more effective than making good decisions. If you think about it, rarely do you ever fully evaluate and learn from your good decisions. You just chalk them up to your native intelligence, wisdom, and natural ability to consider all your options. But you will evaluate your bad decisions and what led you to make them. You will figure out if you let your emotions get the best of you or where your logic broke down. With 20/20 hindsight, you will recognize your poor conclusions and promise yourself not to repeat them. You will have learned. In conclusion, you should be very grateful for all those voices in your head. They make it possible to learn by experience and to gather wisdom.

Peas or Carrots Decision

The Lord appreciates when you ask His counsel, but please note that the Lord may not have an opinion on your question, and He will let you make most of the choices in your life. One evening years ago, we had just blessed our dinner when I had the following conversation with my son Trent, who was then about ten years old:

"Dad, what should I eat first, my peas or carrots?"

"Well, Trent, are you going to eat both of them?" I replied.

"Yes," he responded.

"Then it doesn't matter which you eat first."

"But Dad," he insisted, "which should I eat first?!"

That simple conversation has stuck with me for many years, as I have come to realize there are many peas-or-carrots decisions that we take to our Heavenly Father. In those cases where we insist that God tell us if we should take path A or path B, we should understand the Heavenly Father's response may be something like the following:

> Path A will take you to interesting places. You will meet new people and see new things. You will have moments of great joy and moments of deep sadness. You will have difficulties, but you will develop strengths to overcome them. In the end, you are a faithful child, and I believe you will return to Me in the celestial kingdom.
>
> But the same thing can be said of path B. You will meet different people and see different new things. Path B will also provide moments of joy and sadness unique to that path. But if you choose righteousness, at the end of that path you will still return to Me. My purposes for your earth life are served either way. So what do *you* want to do?

Over the years, I have had many friends who faced important career and family decisions. After days of mulling over their choices, they reported to me that they felt they should choose path B. Since the art of decision-making fascinates me, I have asked them if that conclusion was a result of mental conclusion or spiritual revelation. My most honest friends admitted that they had no idea. I can report the same lack of recognizable revelation in my own life. I have never been able to tell where my mental self ends and my spiritual self begins. I still believe that I made the best career and family decisions I could. Part of our earthly mission is to learn how to use and grow the decision-making capabilities of our brains. Rarely will you get to avoid the responsibility of life decisions by passing them on to your Heavenly Father. After all, you will have to live with all the repercussions of your decisions, so the decision should be yours. Life decisions are difficult but educational, as we shall discuss in the next chapter.

CHAPTER 4

Mental Discipline and Decisions

One of the major changes the Savior made in taking the world from the Old Testament Mosaic law to the gospel of Jesus Christ was requiring we have mental discipline. The Mosaic law only considered your physical actions. You could think whatever thoughts you wanted. But the law of the gospel requires that your thoughts be as clean as your actions. That is a much harder task and requires a dedication to mental discipline. In His Sermon on the Mount, the Lord declared:

> Ye have heard that it is said by them of old time, Thou shalt not kill; and whosoever shall kill shall be in danger of the judgment: But I say unto you, That whosoever is angry with his brother without a cause shall be in danger of the judgment. (Matthew 5:21–22)
> Ye have heard that it was said by them of old time, Thou shalt not commit adultery: But I say unto you, That whosoever looketh on a woman to lust after her hath committed adultery with her already in his heart. (Matthew 5:27–28)

The Savior repeats this commandment in a few other ways as well. We are commanded to "be ye therefore perfect, even as your Father in Heaven is perfect" (Matthew 5:48). One would expect perfection to include mental discipline, since your actions all flow from your mind.

Specifics of this commandment are well illustrated by an event in early Church history. On March 20, 1839, Joseph Smith received the revelation found in Doctrine and Covenants 121. Joseph had been in Liberty Jail for several months by then. From the wording of this section, it is pretty obvious that the Prophet Joseph was frustrated and miserable. He couldn't even stand up completely in his small basement jail cell, and he could only receive visitors for short time periods. The news he received about the Church was discouraging. His people were suffering. In an obviously heart-felt prayer, Joseph pleads that the Lord make right all the illegalities and atrocities that had been visited upon his people. The Lord gives Joseph some beautiful words of encouragement, but He does not agree to right the wrongs at that time (see D&C 121:15). At the end of the revelation, the Lord tells Joseph, "Let thy bowels be also full of charity towards all men, and to the household of faith, and *let virtue garnish thy thoughts unceasingly;* then shalt thy confidence wax strong in the presence of God; and the doctrine of the priesthood shall distill upon thy soul as the dews from heaven" (D&C 121:45; italics added).

What an expectation! Joseph had a lot of free time on his hands and even more anger in his heart. The commandment to "let virtue garnish thy thoughts unceasingly" would be an ongoing battle of the mind. As far as I know, Joseph never reported on his success in letting virtue garnish his thoughts unceasingly. For most of us, only anger and thoughts of revenge would have occupied our minds. But apparently the Lord discourages such thoughts. It seems He expects mental discipline from His children, as indicated by this commandment to Joseph.

Personally, if someone offends me or a member of my family, it takes me days to work through my anger and clear my mind of the future comebacks and criticisms I want to express to them. It takes me a couple of weeks to forgive the offender for being the ignorant, prideful, rude, knuckle-dragging caveman that he appears. (I apologize, but can you see how easy and satisfying that can be?) The admonition given to Joseph to let virtue garnish his thoughts unceasingly seems as close to an impossible commandment as I have ever heard. Even when I am not angry, virtue does not garnish my thoughts unceasingly. I find that people are generally offensive, especially on the road and in airports. Anger makes mental restraint even more difficult. Perhaps considering what is going on in our minds will help us have better mental control.

How Your Emotions Make Decisions

The majority of the most important decisions of your life will affect your future more than your present. For example, a young woman must decide if she wants to go to college after high school. Will that be the happiest path for her to take? Will the diploma be worth all the work of her curriculum of classes? Once graduated, she must choose a job. If she has a

Mental Discipline and Decisions

choice, which job will bring her the most opportunity and career satisfaction? The same questions may be asked of accepting a marriage proposal, moving, buying a house, having children, and which movie to see this weekend. The rational mind will make its contributions to the argument and answer such questions as, "Does your suitor appear to be a good provider? Which job pays the most? Can we afford to pay a mortgage?" But the emotional brain must answer the equally important questions, "What do I feel is the right path? Which choice will make me happy?" You can use your rational mind to choose your career based on which field provides you the best opportunities. Or you can use the emotional side of your brain to choose your career based on what interests you the most. If you are lucky, you can find a job that you love *and* offers exceptional opportunities for growth.

So, how do you use your emotions to make decisions? David Eagleman, author of *The Brain*, has an interesting metaphor: "Time travel is something the human brain does relentlessly. When faced with a decision, our brains simulate different outcomes to generate a mockup of what our future might be. Mentally, we can disconnect from the present moment and voyage to a world that doesn't yet exist . . . Typically, under the radar of awareness, my brain simulates all the options, one at a time, and does a gut check on each."[1]

So, let's say you are at the local deli trying to decide what sandwich you want to eat for lunch. You've narrowed your choices down to a roast beef sandwich with horseradish or a ham sandwich with Dijon mustard. How do you choose? Your rational brain really has little to say about this decision. The sandwiches are equally priced, and either sandwich will satisfy your hunger. The question comes down to what do you feel like eating? To make the decision, your brain actually imagines you biting into the roast beef and horseradish. Then it imagines you taking a bite of the ham and Dijon mustard. Your mind then must decide, "Which simulated bite feels better emotionally?" Your response will be based partially on how pleasurable your latest experiences with roast beef and horseradish or ham and Dijon mustard have been. If you had ham and Dijon during an enjoyable family visit to the zoo last month, then ham and Dijon will have an advantage over the roast beef and horseradish.

Often, your conscious brain will contribute to the decision. If you suddenly remember you left your wallet at home and have no money, you will probably have to leave the deli and forget the sandwich until you have a way to pay for it. Logical decisions featuring facts, numbers, and realities will be made by your rational mind. Emotional decisions are emotional. What shirt should you buy? Should you go on a walk? Which friends do you want to invite for dinner? Answers to longer-term questions like, "What do you want to be when you grow up?" often change over the course of your life, because your brain and emotions mature and reshape themselves. With every experience you have, you become a different person who will make different decisions than the person you were before.

Arguing with Yourself

Mental control is not easy. I have a terrible time exhibiting mental discipline during Church services. Maybe because it is a peaceful, quiet place with only one person speaking at a time, my mind will wander. Usually I can rein it in and return my attention to the speaker. The biggest challenge occurs when the speaker mentions a perspective that I have not thought about before. Without prompting, my mind will start to make new connections of relevant facts, good metaphors, or other arguments around a gospel topic that I have been contemplating. It is so exciting when such epiphanies occur—but they are also very distracting. My mind starts having an argument with itself. If you could hear the debate inside my head, it might sound something like this:

> "We have to record this thought. Pull out your cell phone and open up the Notes app."
>
> "No, we're sitting in church. People will think I am answering my email!"
>
> "We're never going to remember this line of reasoning. Pull out your cell phone and record this new perspective!"
>
> "I am surrounded by friends and family. Pulling out my phone will set a bad example!"
>
> "But this is such a great thought. We'll forget it by the time church is over!"
>
> "Quiet! I cannot focus on this talk and I am not feeling the Spirit."
>
> "We're going to forget. We're going to forget. We're going to forget."

Obviously, I need more mental discipline. But the point of this example is that you can't learn the gospel effectively if your mind is too distracted or tired to incorporate what is being taught. We are on earth to gain knowledge and choose righteously.[2] If you miss opportunities to pull knowledge into your mind, then you are missing a main point of earth life. Your brain can be a wonderful tool in achieving the spiritual knowledge you seek—or it can be your worst distraction. Usually, it's both. In any case, learn as much as you can.

How to Make Decisions with Prayer

It should not be surprising that the discussion on quality prayers should be in the chapter on mental discipline. With our rational brain, we evaluate the logic and reason behind a decision. One part of your mind may ask, "Is alternative A illegal, or does it break a commandment?" Another part may ask, "Could alternative B be potentially dangerous or financially damaging?" A tired part of your brain may worry, "Will alternative C involve a lot more work than the others?"

At the same time, your emotional brain starts its evaluation of the decision. We think forward in time, predicting how we feel emotionally about each option. A part of your brain may respond, "But won't the extra work of alternative C be worth the joy it brings?" A more compassionate part of your brain may ask, "Will any of these choices be better for our children or other people we love? Which choice will make all our lives happier?"

With this firestorm of thoughts going on in your head, you might decide to pray about the decision. In the many church lessons I have received about prayer, the class is provided with a checklist that includes directives to "find a quiet place to pray, kneel, and clear your mind. Then you just need to . . ."

"Wait a second," I always want to interrupt. "I have real difficulties clearing my mind." The thoughts that keep coming in from all different parts of my brain don't respectfully stop for me so I can take a moment in prayer. The part of my brain that suggested a prayer doesn't seem to have any authority over the rest of my mind. Part of my brain is saying, "Let us pray," but the other parts continue their discussions (somewhat like the beginning of many family dinners).

This is when many people think they can discipline their brain to do what it should. The part of your mind that wants to pray has certainly made a good choice. But to accomplish the task, it must demand that all the other parts of the brain stop thinking and listen to the prayer. If you have a well-disciplined mind, then perhaps such a request will work. But for the rest of us, our mind keeps on thinking. For example, have you ever gotten a favorite song stuck in your head? Can you turn it off when you kneel down to pray?

Your spiritual self cannot bully your mental self into submission. In all these situations, one must simply have patience. Wait long enough and the song stuck in your head will go away. If you have just learned about a major decision you must make, give your mind time to think it through. If it is a sudden and significant decision, you probably have some adrenaline, a bit of stress, and anxiety working their way through your brain right now. Every part of the mental council in your mind is going to want to resolve this issue as soon as possible. So, let your brain wrestle with the issue to exhaustion. Let every part of your mind make its suggestions and the other parts of the brain dismiss those suggestions as poor ideas. You might want to talk to someone who loves you enough to listen to you ramble on about the possible ramifications of each choice. In any case, let your mind calm down and reduce the number of potential solutions. You will have less trouble clearing your conscious mind and offering a coherent prayer for help.

Before offering a prayer for help to make a complex decision, it is often best to break that decision down to a very few paths forward. It is often easiest if the prayer is in the form of a yes/no confirmation so the answer does not involve a detailed, worded response. Richard G. Scott explained, "I know the reality of the promptings of the Holy Ghost. In times of urgent need, after meditation and prayer to receive confirmation of a selected course of action, those promptings have given the comforted feeling that it was right."[3]

This requires thought and decisions. If you have not made a decision on what you want to do, then how are you going to ask for confirmation of what you have decided?

Oliver Cowdery received a revelation through Joseph Smith that further confirms the requirement to engage our mental process before our spiritual process. We read, "Behold, you have not understood; you have supposed that I would give it unto you, when *you took no thought* save it was to ask me. But, behold, I say unto you, that you *must study it out in your mind*; then you must ask me if it be right, and if it is right I will cause that your bosom should burn within you; therefor you shall feel that it is right" (D&C 9:7–8; italics added).

In this section, the Lord was giving counsel to Oliver on how to translate. Oliver was being given instruction to study a section of text

Mental Discipline and Decisions

needing translation, come up with his best interpretation, and ask the Lord if it was correct. Then he would receive his answer. In church discussions today, we apply this revelation to much more than how to translate ancient texts. The instruction is sound, of course, but Oliver's question was fairly black and white. The translation was either right or it wasn't. When we are praying about something that has multiple options and no obvious "right" or "wrong" answer, decisions get harder. Where should you go to college? Which job should you accept or which house should you buy?

Your own perception of your Heavenly Father is important in these kinds of prayer. After you have laid out the problem with its possible choices and solutions, please know that the first thing your Heavenly Father will ask is, "Well what do *you* want to do?" When the brother of Jared asked the Lord about getting light into their ships for their voyage across the ocean, the Lord asked him (*twice*), "What will ye that I should do that ye may?" (Ether 2:23, 25). This is not an uncommon response from the Lord. It's your life, so what do you want to do with it? What do you want the Lord to do for you, besides taking upon Himself the burden of making your decisions?

After days of mentally contemplating a big change in your life, you may start to view it as the most important question of your mortal existence. The choice may appear as if it will be a major turning point in your life (which it could be) and your single opportunity for life success (which it is not). We often take that mental anxiety into our prayers with us and wonder why God is not giving us the pyrotechnic answer it deserves. It is at this point that we need to remember that God takes the longer view on your decisions than you probably do. He wants you to be a good decision maker and may see your upcoming choice as a good opportunity for you to work on that skill. God gave you a working brain to make these exact decisions in your life. It would be a shame not to use it.

ENDNOTES

1. David Eagleman, *The Brain* (New York: Pantheon Books, 2015), 117.
2. Scott R. Frazer, *Angry with God* (Springville, UT: Cedar Fort Publishing, 2020).
3. Richard G. Scott, "Gratitude," April 1977 general conference, churchofjesuschrist.org/general-conference/1977/04?lang=eng.

CHAPTER 5

Neuroplasticity and Repentance

The word *repentance* is translated from the Greek word *metanoia*, which is a compound word that means "to think differently after." So, repentance and its Greek root mean to change your way of thinking. We may believe that repentance means leaving behind bad habits and doing good. But repentance goes both ways—you can just as easily repent of good works as bad. I was nice to my neighbor yesterday, but I've repented of that and won't do it again.

As already defined, your brain has a capability called neuroplasticity (neuro, for nerves and plasticity for shapable or moldable), which makes repentance possible. When you repent, neuroplasticity allows your brain to adjust its thinking to the new conduct. If you return to church attendance after a time of inactivity, your brain will gradually make the newfound fellowship less awkward. You will remember your past learnings about the gospel.

This understanding of the brain's ability to change itself has not always been recognized by the medical community. Nerve cells, whether they are in your leg or your brain, heal more slowly than muscle or skin cells. In fact, they heal so slowly that for years the medical community believed that the brain was incapable of healing itself at all. It was thought that mental handicaps and brain injuries were permanent and any treatments were probably a waste of time. After its development during childhood, the medical profession believed that the only change to the adult brain was its slow decline to old age and dementia. Medical students were taught that brains, like computers, were "hardwired." Brain surgeons removed tumors such that the brain could hopefully return to its baseline functionality, but no one believed the brain could fix itself. The feeling was that your thought processes became set in stone with age and, as the saying goes, "You can't teach an old dog new tricks."

But this opinion flew in the face of repentance, one of the core tenets of Christianity. We have multiple scriptures that encourage us to repent. One such scripture says, "Behold, he who has repented of his sins, the same is forgiven, and I, the Lord, remember them no more. By this ye may know if a man repenteth of his sins—behold, he will confess them and forsake them" (D&C 58:42–43).

For a man to forsake his sins, he has to change the way he thinks. The Savior made that fact clear in the Sermon on the Mount when He taught that His new gospel required you to control your thoughts as well as your actions. You should not kill, nor even be angry with your brother. You should not commit adultery, nor even look lustfully upon a woman. Before, you could hate your enemies, but now you need to love your enemies and bless them that curse you. Imagine the changes that early Church members had to make in response to the teachings of the Savior.

If the brain was really hardwired and could not be changed, repentance would be impossible. To start the repentance process, you must believe that you *can* change your brain, you *can* change your thought patterns, and you *can* reduce the temptations that afflict you. Fortunately, over the years, medical science changed its stance on the brain. Dr. Norman Doidge, author of *The Brain that Changes Itself*, explained the history of this new attitude toward brain flexibility. In the early 1970s, brain researchers made a series of unexpected discoveries. "They showed that the brain changed its very structure with each different activity it performed, perfecting its circuits so it was better suited to the task at hand. If certain "parts" failed, then other parts could sometimes take over. . . . They began to call this fundamental brain property 'neuroplasticity.'"[1]

Neuroplasticity is a blessing because it allows us to repent. To change our lives and forsake old, unrighteous patterns, we have to change our way of thinking about our priorities, our goals, and the sins that oppose us in achieving the way of life that we desire. So, how does our brain make those changes?

Memories

Each of your memories is represented in your brain as a particular pattern of firing neurons. Your conscious brain recognizes a given pattern as a friend's face or the lyrics of a song. You may have millions of neurons that can be used to make these recognizable patterns. Each neuron is often required to multitask and be involved in more than one memory. Neurons from one memory may be recruited to participate in other memories. So the patterns of old memories can start to become muddled. Neurons that have been reprogrammed no longer participate to form the patterns of fading memories. As discussed, very emotional memories tend to be longer-lived than non-emotional memories. But in either case, "the enemy of memory isn't time; it's other memories."[2]

Old memories must fade away. It is a gradual process, of course, but it is also necessary. Though you may curse your memory when you forget the name of a friend you haven't seen for years or the new neighbor you just met yesterday, we should still be thankful for the ability to forget. We want the memories of traumatic events to fade away. Our past should be replaced by our present. If you don't have a way to clear out old memories, you will continue to live in your most carefree past and fail to move on to your next phase of life. As Paul explained it, "When I was a child, I spake as a child, I understood as a child, I thought as a child: but when I became a man, I put away childish things" (1 Corinthians 13:11).

So, the first part of neuroplasticity and repentance is to forget old ways. You can keep your most treasured memories by bringing them to mind occasionally to reinforce their patterns. But know that the memories you would like to forget *will* fade away as you overlay them with new and, hopefully, much better memories.

Ingraining New Thought Patterns

When reading is taught to children, it changes the biological structure of their brains. Reading changes neuron connections since memories of letters and words must be created and stored. The "angular and supra-marginal gyrus" link the different parts of the brain together to allow us to read. But the changes caused by learning to read flow throughout other brain modules as well. Amazingly, in just a few months, a child can learn to read. Major changes to their thought patterns are made in a very short time. Fortunately, the skills you learn as a child—walking, reading, swimming, and biking—will stay with you throughout your life. But opinion, habits, temptations, and biases will change over your lifetime. You may have arrived at an age that requires you to think more seriously about eating healthy foods and exercising more. The current political environment may have changed your opinions about your political party and national leaders. You may have not attended church for many years and are thinking it is time to return.

For most of your life, your brain will allow you to make such changes. It has the plasticity to make changes in the way you think, which is important because repentance is all about changing your life's direction. But, please note, neuroplasticity does diminish with age. Like the joints and muscles of your body, the brain also loses it flexibility. "As we age and plasticity declines, it becomes increasingly difficult for us to change in response to the world, even if we want to. We find familiar types of stimulation pleasurable; we seek out like-minded individuals to associate with, and research shows we tend to ignore or forget or attempt to discredit information that does not match our beliefs."[3]

Thus, the possibility of your death isn't the only reason that you should "not procrastinate the day of your repentance" (Alma 13:27). As you enter into your elderly years, the capacity of your brain to repent and change its thought patterns is actually reduced. Being able to change your mind is a blessing that allows you to both gather wisdom and modify poor behaviors.

Your Brain Will Adjust

Once again, I would like to address the conscious mind of my reader (though I have been doing so throughout the whole book). Conscious mind, you have to have confidence in your brain's ability to adjust to whatever changes you choose to make. For example, you may wish to give up an addiction—let's say smoking. For several days, your brain will rebel. From the time you started smoking, nicotine has been bonding to your acetylcholine receptors, activating the reward circuit and producing calm. Because there was so much nicotine around, your brain adjusted to it by producing less acetylcholine and reducing the number of acetylcholine receptors. If you quit smoking and stop providing nicotine, your acetylcholine neurotransmitter system will be disrupted yet again. You will feel anxiety and discomfort for several days. But your brain *will* figure it out. It will produce more acetylcholine and increase the number of its receptors. Gradually, your brain will return to its normal, nicotine-free functionality.

The brain can also recover from other addictions, be they other drugs, pornography, or video games. If you wish, you can learn to speak without using profanity. If you choose to try, you can learn to attend church on Sundays. Granted, guiding your brain into new thought patterns is almost always difficult. Your brain doesn't normally like change; it is much more comfortable following the routine patterns it has already etched into your mind. There is an uncomfortable learning curve in any new endeavor. Thus, repentance is not easy. Almost all changes in life are like quitting smoking—you are bound to feel anxiety and discomfort in your initial efforts.

Our Savior and the Church leaders want to continually encourage you to repent of your disobedience to the commandments, as you will have more joy if you do. Thus, a significant portion of the scriptures and latter-day teachings center on repentance. Your mind often needs encouragement to change your thoughts, so Church leaders from Adam to the present day have tried to provide such persuasion. Help is always available from the Church, friends, and family to support your search for happiness.

To repeat, the discomfort you may feel in repentance—be it quitting smoking or returning to church activity—is your brain resisting the change. Yes, your brain will whine and complain and you may think, "I can't do this." But be patient, because you and your brain can indeed do this. Like a child's brain learns to read, your brain will make its needed adjustments.

Neuroplasticity and Agency

Neuroplasticity also guarantees you your agency. Your brain will continue to change and mold itself into any patterns to which you choose to expose it. Those patterns can be good habits, or they can be detrimental to your future happiness. We briefly reviewed the effects of social media and the internet. The more time you spend on email, video games, and social media, the better you will get at them. You will become more adept at living in the virtual world and less capable of living in the real world. In a future chapter, we will discuss drug and sensorial addictions. For now, please recognize that the neuroplasticity that allows your brain to repent will also allow you to return to old habits as well. You were born on this earth to be tested and tried. Your brain and spirit get to make choices, and your brain is designed to vigorously pursue those decisions, be they good or evil.

Neuroplasticity should give you hope. Wherever your brain is now, whatever you find yourself thinking, you *can* change it. But realize that your brain can return to making bad decisions, should you choose to allow it. You will always have your agency.

ENDNOTES

1. Doidge, *The Brain that Changes Itself,* xviii.
2. Eagleman, *The Brain*, 24.
3. Doidge, *The Brain that Changes Itself,* 304.

CHAPTER 6

The Physical, Mental, and Spiritual

Hopefully you will have noticed a recurring theme in this book that our physical, mental, and spiritual selves are connected and dependent on one another. God understands that fact, of course. So, though He mostly works with our spiritual side, Heavenly Father gave us a number of commandments that focus on maintaining our physical and mental health as well. We have general commandments about maintaining good health (see D&C 42:43, D&C 89:18) and some that are more specific, including this advice on when to sleep: "Cease to be idle; cease to be unclean; cease to find fault one with another; cease to sleep longer than is needful; retire to thy bed early, that ye may not be weary; arise early, that your bodies and your minds may be invigorated" (D&C 88:124).

So, before proceeding further, let's spend some time considering how our mental, physical, and spiritual states actually interact with one other. Much of what we do in our worship is done to put us in the right mentality for the spiritual connections we seek. We need to reconsider old traditions about our worship and understand what helps and what hinders spirituality.

The Mentality of Pain

Repentance is a complex practice and not well understood by many faithful Christians even today. The main purpose of repentance is to change our proclivity toward sin. The goal is to cause a change in us so we don't want to seek unrighteous living. After recognizing our sins, the next step of repentance is to feel remorseful about them. Throughout religious history, some people have been so remorseful that they sought to cause themselves real physical pain as part of their repentance. The

53

logic was that if you learn to associate sin with discomfort or agony, you would be less likely to misbehave. In the fourteenth century, self-flagellation became such a popular practice among its members that the Catholic Church had to issue a decree forbidding it. Unbelievably, the activity is still accomplished in many parts of the world, especially around Easter time in recognition of the suffering of the Savior. The idea that physical pain somehow absolves us of sin has continued, despite the many church teachings against it. In considering your sins, you should feel some mental anguish—but you are most certainly not supposed to feel physical pain.

The "mortification" of the body (recommended in Romans 8:13 and Colossians 3:5) means to subdue or overcome the desires of the body by self-denial and self-discipline. Some religions and people have taken this concept to its extreme, thinking that physical punishment will cause the body to resist sin. But the idea makes no sense. You cannot "beat some sense" into yourself or anyone else. Self-discipline is a worthy goal, but the means to accomplish it must be based on mental dedication and not physical pain. Pain distracts the mind from its tasks; it does not focus it.

Thus, in all spiritual pursuits, pain should be avoided. If your knees are arthritic, do not feel the need to kneel in prayer. You may think that withstanding the pain of kneeling and demonstrating humility will be noted and appreciated by God. But this is never the kind of sacrifice that He wants from you. When you are ill, restoring your health should be your top priority, well ahead of observing the Sabbath and temple attendance. In fact, temple and stake leaders will beg you to refrain from attending any Church services when you are sick. (This counsel has become especially important in the present day of avoiding COVID-19.) Not only do you endanger the health of other Church members, but you really cannot increase your spirituality when you are physically ill. Staying home and recovering your health is a higher commandment than observing the Sabbath by attending Church services.

The Mentality of Fasting

Fasting is the one form of self-denial that is practiced regularly by numerous religions today. The Savior fasted at the beginning of His ministry to spiritually prepare and strengthen Himself for His ministry. Fasting is an interesting intersection of your spiritual, mental, and physical selves. Your mental side makes the decision to fast, a determination that is strengthened and encouraged by your spiritual side. After about six hours, your physical self—your body—will start to recognize that it requires nourishment, and hunger pangs will be relayed from your stomach to your brain. But your mental self remembers the spiritually based decision it has reached. It tries to ignore the physical promptings of the body, even as those promptings become more intense.

I have heard teachings that fasts are designed to overcome temptations of the physical body. But it is actually your mind that succumbs to temptations, not your body. Granted, you can train your mind to resist hunger. But this accomplishment does not necessarily strengthen your ability to resist other temptations of the flesh—or mind. The presumption of mortification, or subduing of bodily desires, is that your body must be subjugated and brought to heel by the spirit. The belief is that physical pain will more quickly bring about self-discipline. Fasting is meant to bring about some physical weakness. Humility comes with the realization that a few hours without food makes even the strongest man weak and distracted. Taking the verse quite literally, we are counseled to not "put trust in the arm of flesh" (2 Nephi 4:34). Though having a strong body is good, fasting is designed to help us realize that this physical strength is fleeting.

But a distinction must be made here. Fasting can lead one to a heightened spirituality, but it is not meant to be painful. Fasts are not supposed to be longer than twenty-four hours for a good reason.[1] First, longer fasts are unhealthy for your body. Second, after a full day of going without food or water, the fast is working at cross purposes to your spirituality. The brain becomes lethargic from the lack of glucose in the bloodstream. It becomes too distracted by feelings of hunger being sent to it from your body to allow significant spiritual communication. If you are ill, you should shorten your fast. If you have developed a health condition, are pregnant, or have reached an age where fasting has become a painful burden, fasts should be shorter still. Fasting is done to demonstrate sacrifice, but it is sacrifice for the purpose of increased spirituality and communion with God. If the length of a fast has exceeded that purpose, then it should be discontinued. Your Heavenly Father will not be impressed by a fast that lasts longer than Church recommendations. In summary, fasts are not designed to punish your body for its ego and temptations. Fasts are *not* designed to so weaken the body that the spiritual self can "take control." Fasts are designed to demonstrate to the mind that physical strength diminishes quickly without God's blessing of food. It is the humility that comes with this realization that allows more spiritual prayers after a fast.

The Mentality of Prayer

Spirituality is rather impossible to distinguish in other people, and I have never understood how one person can ever describe someone else as a spiritual person. From what physical evidence can one person make such a claim? We can observe that a faithful friend is very pious and makes every effort to put themselves into spiritual situations, such as the temple, church meetings, and so on. But environment is only half of the equation for feeling the Spirit. As most all of us have experienced, you can put yourself into a very spiritual setting and not feel the Spirit. Unless you are able to clear your turbulent mind and prepare yourself mentally, there is actually little hope of feeling the Spirit. So, it seems that a spiritual person is actually someone who regularly makes an effort to put themselves into a spiritual setting and, at the same time, achieves a calm and repentant mindset. Spirituality is so dependent on your mental state that the only person who can really judge your own spirituality is you.

Since childhood, we have been taught the basics of preparing our environment and minds for spiritual communication. For example, if you are going to pray, you are counseled to find a quiet, peaceful place to do so. This is not because noise drives away the Holy Ghost. It is because you don't have the mental discipline to prevent the noise from distracting you. But seeking to put yourself into the right frame of mind for prayer goes beyond finding a quiet place. Why do we fold our arms and close our eyes when praying? It prevents our senses of touch and sight from distracting our mind. Why do we kneel and bow our heads? Because it helps us get into the proper mental attitude for our prayer. When we kneel, we demonstrate both our humility and trust in the Lord. By kneeling, we recognize that we are in the presence of a greater power. We do not stand as equals. Also, when kneeling and bowing your head, you put yourself into a very physically vulnerable position. If a blow is to come, you are not in a position to block it or even move out of the way. Thus we show our trust in the Lord and symbolically demonstrate that we will accept whatever judgment He will make.

On the other hand, we do not prostrate ourselves by lying on our stomach with our face to the floor. This is more a position of humiliation rather than a demonstration of humility. We are not groveling before the Lord; we are, after all, His sons and daughters. The Lord does not need us to kneel before Him in prayer. The kneeling, however, puts us in the right frame of mind to better deliver our prayer and receive an answer.

The Physical, Mental, and Spiritual

Receiving answers to prayer requires even greater mental focus. First we allow our own thoughts to come forward for the Lord to review. We must then try to silence our thoughts on the decision and open ourselves up to any spiritual revelations that the Lord might provide. Prayer becomes a deliberate mediation in choosing our best path forward. It is one of the most deliberate combinations that your mental and spiritual selves will make. In our lessons and discussions about the Holy Ghost, we often refer to communication from the Spirit as a "still small voice" (see 1 Kings 19:11–12, 1 Nephi 17:45, D&C 85:6). There are a few problems with this simile. First and foremost, please note that only rarely is the still, small voice actually a voice. Personally, I have never heard a voice giving me instruction during a prayer. Those who have heard a voice (usually either encouraging or warning them) generally admit that it has happened only once or twice in their lives. The impressions we receive from the Holy Ghost are almost always thoughts, not voices. Thus, from the beginning of our prayers to their end, we need to put our minds in the proper state to most effectively pray. We will return to this theme again—your spiritual state always depends on your mental state. Most all of the rituals that we perform before a prayer are designed to put us into the proper mindset for that prayer. If your brain is overworked, overstimulated, or overstressed, spiritual communication becomes very difficult.

The Mentality of Worship

For nearly two millennia after its founding, the Catholic Church built massive cathedrals for its Church services and worship. Enormous stained glass windows added an ethereal, heavenly glow to the sunlight streaming in. These huge cathedrals were built to promote awe and humility in anyone who entered. The church wanted its members to understand that God is so great, His cathedrals must be enormous. It was believed that awe and humility would best prepare members for a deep spiritual experience. Today, religions have taken a less grandiose approach to building cathedrals and church buildings. Our culture has changed, and thus so has our mentality toward our church buildings. We don't want to feel insignificant in God's presence. We want to feel that God is our loving Heavenly Father. Church chapels are smaller, simpler, and generally designed for noise suppression. Our latter-day temples are beautiful but simply decorated. Most Christians now associate this newer decor with Sabbath worship. The mentality of our worship has changed.

57

Some people declare that going into the mountains to commune with God is their form of worship. This is fine, as nature is so beautiful that we can more fully appreciate God's creations while there. But nowhere in the scriptures is nature recommended as a place for formal worship services. For worship, God wants you to enjoy the fellowship and support of other members—not to be alone. Second, nature is often so beautiful it can be distracting. Your attention can easily change from listening to a teacher to watching the passing clouds. Nature is great for personal prayer, as Joseph Smith discovered, but it is not a great place for creating the right mentality for congregational worship. Thus we are blessed to have chapels and meetinghouses in which to gather, fellowship, and learn.

The Mentality of the Word of Wisdom

We tend to think of the Word of Wisdom as a commandment to maintain good physical health. This is true, of course. But in considering the commandment, we should recognize that it is mainly designed to help us to maintain good mental health. Your body from the neck down does *not* become addicted to alcohol, tobacco, cocaine, or similar drugs. But your brain certainly does.

Thus, as one might expect, the Word of Wisdom promises mental blessings as well as physical benefits from following its counsel: "And all Saints who remember to keep and do these sayings, walking in obedience to the commandments, shall receive health in their navel and marrow in their bones: And shall *find wisdom and great treasures of knowledge*, even hidden treasures; And shall run and not be weary, and shall walk and not faint" (D&C 89:18–20; italics added).

We were given the Word of Wisdom to help maintain our minds and bodies, because only through good physical and mental health can we find spiritual connection. Millions of chemical reactions are going on inside your brain this very moment. Your brain chemistry is a delicate balance, and certain foods, drinks, and drugs can severely interrupt that balance. Your Heavenly Father wants your brain to stay as clear as possible. Thus He has given us directives on how to maintain the health of your body and mind. The Word of Wisdom is simply one of those directives.

The point of this chapter is that we should work with our brain in seeking spiritual connection with our Heavenly Father. We should recognize those distractions that will sidetrack our brains (pain, noise, distracting environment, fatigue, drugs) and seek to remove them if at all

The Physical, Mental, and Spiritual

possible. Rarely does it really work to try to "power through" a prayer despite outside interferences. Prayer requires your brain to focus its full attention on it. One should always seek to cooperate with the brain in accomplishing your goals.

With that being said, we are now going to take a few chapters to discuss the brain/spirit interaction. To do so, we must better define some words, most of which have been misused for centuries. In order, let's consider the heart, spirit, soul, our consciousness, and then our conscience.

ENDNOTE

1. *General Handbook: Serving in The Church of Jesus Christ of Latter-day Saints*, Section 38.8.19; churchofjesuschrist.org/study/manual/general-handbook/38—church-policies-and-guidelines?lang=eng.

CHAPTER 7

Understanding the Heart Metaphor

According to the search function of my electronic scriptures, the word *heart* is used an astonishing 1,654 times in the standard works. That is twice as many usages as the word *prayer* and three times as many as the word *obey*. It is by far the most used metaphor of the scriptures. It is used so much that we forget that that this scriptural heart does not really mean our beating heart. If your father tells you, "It's the love in your heart that matters," he will probably tap his left breast, as if that is where we store love. We are just so wrapped up in the metaphor that we forget that our spiritual "hearts" are not really in our chests.

The history of the word *heart* in the scriptures is really quite interesting. For centuries, the heart metaphor for our spiritual center was not even a metaphor. In the fourth century BC, Aristotle identified the heart as the most important organ of the body and where our thoughts and emotions were generated. George Sarton wrote, "Aristotle considered the heart the seat of intelligence, the function of the brain being simply to cool the heart by the secretion of Phlegm and to prevent its overheating. . . . Aristotle's position was clear: the brain may serve the mind indirectly (by its action upon the heart), but it is not the seat of reason."[1]

The concept that the heart was the center of reason, emotion, and spirituality continued for hundreds of years. Even by the late twelfth century, the heart was considered to be the primary "spiritual member" of the body and, thus, the origin of all emotions. This perception was being taught in all the finest schools of the time. The heart was, after all, the first organ that one can see developing in a growing embryo. Unless they had received a special revelation on human anatomy, the authors of our scriptures almost certainly believed that the heart was

61

the source of our spiritual selves and the place where thoughts and emotions reside.

But as early as 500 BC, a fellow Greek philosopher named Alcmaeon taught that all senses are connected to the brain.[2] Around 400 BC, the Greek physician and philosopher Hippocrates reiterated that the brain was the center of our thoughts and emotions. Despite their evidence, these conclusions were pretty much ignored for centuries. Finally, in 1628, the English physician William Harvey reported that the heart is actually a recirculating pump for our blood, made of a special type of muscle.[3] It holds no memories. Eventually scientists provided enough data to convince the world that the brain really is the center of thought and decision making. But the image of the heart being the center of our emotions and feelings has continued to this day.

In these modern times, we know a lot more about the human body than Aristotle. Though clarification is probably unnecessary, your doctor and the medical community will assure you that the heart is a four-chambered pump that moves blood throughout the body. Obviously, this is an important function that allows you to live. Blood carries oxygen from the lungs and nutrients from the stomach to keep cells alive from your brain to your toes. It then carries carbon dioxide and other waste products from those cells to your lungs and kidneys, respectively, for proper disposal. I don't want to take anything away from the heart. The heart is an incredible organ. The contraction of the heart and the coordination with its valves is simply astonishing.[4] If you have an average heart rate of eighty beats per minute and you live to be eighty years old, your heart will conduct this coordination of valves and muscles a total of 3.6 billion times.

However, despite its critical importance to our lives, we have to understand that the heart is a muscle. It has no brain tissue to store memories, ponder, or think. So, though early Christian writers perhaps didn't realize that the heart wasn't the thinking, spiritual organ in our bodies, we should fully understand it today. When you read the word *heart* in the scriptures, you should realize it is almost always used as a metaphor. For simplicity, we will use the term "scriptural heart" to refer to your spiritual side, and "beating heart" in reference to the organ that moves blood through your body.

In retrospect, it is too bad the heart does not actually contain our love for our families and our spirituality. After all, this perception has a very well-organized feeling to it. The brain could be considered our on-board computer, containing all the memories and thought processes we will ever need. The heart, which is located about twelve inches away from the brain, could be considered our emotional center, where we hold our emotions and spiritual communication with God. However untrue, this separation of the two most critical aspects of our lives seems like such a good idea. Who would want our logical thoughts, illogical emotions, and deep spiritual feelings interfering with each other in the same location? It would be chaos. However, we now know that this is exactly what is going on inside of our heads.

The Scriptural Heart

Though our beating heart is not the heart mentioned so many times in the scriptures, there should be no doubt that the "scriptural heart" still exists. Its use in the scriptures, hymns, and classical literature over the centuries is so pervasive we shouldn't doubt its existence today. Millions of people have recognized and testified about their own spiritual centers, which makes it hard to dismiss them all as imaginary. The "heart" defined in our scriptures exists, though defining it has always been difficult.

Fortunately, there are many scriptures about the scriptural heart, and one can get a pretty good description of it. As you read the following descriptions of the heart taken from the scriptures, try to imagine what they might actually be describing:

- Your heart can be pure (Matthew 5:8), meek, or lowly (Matthew 11:29).
- Your heart can harden (Mark 6:52) and wax gross (Matthew 13:15).
- Out of the heart comes the things we say (Matthew 12:34).
- You can think with your heart (Luke 9:47, Matthew 9:4) and make decisions there (Luke 21:14).
- You can say things to yourself in your heart (Matthew 24:48, 1 Nephi 4:10, Mosiah 4:24).
- You can understand with your heart (Matthew 13:15).
- You can lay plans in your heart (Alma 47:4).
- You can doubt (Mark 11: 23), ponder (Luke 2:19, 1 Nephi 11:1), and muse (Luke 3:15) in your heart.
- Your heart can reason (Luke 5:22, Mark 2:6), be troubled (John 14:1), and remember.
- Your heart can be heavy and have continual sorrow (Romans 9:2).

- Your heart can be opened (Acts 16:14) or your heart can hold secrets (1 Corinthians 14:25).
- The hearts of the simple can be deceived (Romans 16:18).
- Finally, out of the heart proceed evil thoughts, murders, adulteries, fornications, thefts, false witness, and blasphemies (Matthew 15:19).

These descriptions make the heart sound very much like the mind. The beating heart can do none of the above tasks. But the mind can. Only your mind can reason, doubt, remember, or think. Only out of your brain proceeds evil thoughts, murders, false witness, and blasphemies. You can harden your mind against all good advice. In fact, your mind is the only part of you that can hope to accomplish any of the above actions.

So, does God care about what you are thinking in your mind? The next time you read your scriptures, every time you see the word *heart*, substitute in the word *mind*. For example, "And God saw that the wickedness of man was great in the earth, and that every imagination of the thoughts of his heart was only evil continually" (Genesis 6:5).

Once you realize how many times the Lord refers to your mind in the scriptures, you will be convinced that the Lord cares very much about what is going on inside your head.

What Is Our Spiritual Heart?

Authors of the scriptures often used the word *heart* instead of the word *mind*, which somewhat muddied the waters as far as its definition. Putting that confusion aside for a moment, what concept are we trying to communicate when we talk about our non-physical "heart"? Certainly, the scriptural heart includes emotions and spiritual yearnings to know God. But the word *heart* was not meant to include *all* our brain. It doesn't include the conscious parts of your brain that you use to remember grocery lists, drive a car through a crowded parking lot, or read a romance novel. It doesn't include the unconscious parts of our brain that helps you swing a golf club or keep your heart beating. No, the scriptural heart is your emotional center or the core of your very being. It provides the natural inclinations of what you immediately want to do in any given situation. Sometimes after thinking something through, your logical mind will convince your core being to modify your first inclinations. Often this is a good change; sometimes it's not.

I found the modern equivalent of the spiritual heart in two books called *The Happiness Hypothesis* and *The Righteous Mind* by Jonathan Haidt. Haidt establishes an interesting metaphor to explain the brain. He suggests that the mind can be thought of as an elephant and its rider. The elephant represents your automatic processes, including emotion, reaction, and intuition. The rider represents your controlled processes, which are made up of reasoning and logical processing.

Despite his conscious mind telling him what he *should* do, Haidt realized that he only rarely listened to that advice and would generally do what his emotions wanted him to do. In describing this weakness of will, Haidt relates the following metaphor, with the voice of his conscious mind: "The image that I came up for myself, as I marveled at my weakness, was that I was a rider on the back of an elephant. I'm holding the reins in my hands, and by pulling one way or the other I can tell the elephant to turn, to stop, or to go. I can direct things, but only when the elephant doesn't have any desires of his own. When the elephant really wants to do something, I'm no match for him."[5]

For example, as a parent, if you hear your young daughter cry out, your initial inclination is to rush to her aid. You love your daughter and this reaction emanates from the very core of your being. The elephant in you immediately turns from what you were doing to rush to the aid of your child. But then the rider of the elephant reminds you that your daughter is playing downstairs with friends. Screams are rather common when these girls get together, and perhaps rushing to her aid is not required. You pause and then hear a chorus of giggles and more screams. The rider was right; there was nothing to fear.

We often think that our emotions get in the way of clear thinking. One of my all-time favorite television series was the original *Star Trek*. The entire pointed-ear population of the planet Vulcan, represented on the starship *Enterprise* by Mr. Spock, had come to the conclusion that emotions had to be banished from their thought process and decisions. They all sought to think and make choices based on pure logic. So, do emotions really cloud our thinking? Does the emotional elephant get in the way of its logical, clear-thinking rider?

Some people, due to a stroke, brain tumor, or blow to the head, have lost function in a part of their frontal cortex. This disengages the part of the brain that processes emotion. When they should feel intense emotion, they report feeling nothing. Do they become like Mr. Spock, whose cold deduction saved the ship and its crew in multiple episodes? Actually, they don't. Instead, those who have disengaged their emotions due to depression or a damaged cortex have a much harder time making decisions. Without the emotional response to immediately eliminate most options, people without sentiment must logically sort through all of them. Decisions become overwhelming. We need both the emotional and caring heart and the reasoning logical mind to make decisions. As Haidt concludes, "Human rationality depends critically on sophisticated emotionality. It is only because our emotional brains work so well that our reasoning can work at all."[6]

When the scriptures mention the spiritual heart, I believe they are mostly talking about your core mindset, your emotions, and your internal principles (or the elephant) in each one of us. The Lord wants us to endeavor to make our inner self, our emotions, and initial reactions righteous and charitable. When a temptation makes itself known, your initial response should be to walk away. When you see someone in need, your first reaction should be to help. The conscious mind (or elephant rider) may warn you to think about what you are doing for a moment. Since your initial reactions may put you in danger, you should listen to it. But hopefully your initial reaction to any question in your life is the right and righteous thing to do. If it is, then you can and should follow your heart. Your emotions, your logical mind, and your spiritual heart can all work together to prompt you in the right direction.

The Stirrings of the Holy Ghost

Part of the confusion in identifying the heart metaphor is that the heart, rather strangely, is often the place where we feel the stirrings of the Holy Ghost. The Lord said, "But, behold, I say unto you, that you must study it out in your mind; then you must ask me if it be right, and if it is right I will cause that your bosom shall burn within you; therefore, you shall feel that it is right" (D&C 9:8).

Numerous other scriptures also refer to people feeling a burning within their hearts due to the testimony of the spirit (see Luke 24:32, 3 Nephi 11:3). Many members of the Church have felt those stirrings and have struggled to adequately describe them. It is both fascinating and hard to fathom just why the Holy Ghost manifests itself in this way.

In giving my testimony one Sunday, I mentioned my thoughts around the interaction of the Holy Ghost with our bodies. I suggested that the

Spirit witnesses to our whole body and we actually feel it in the center of our mass, somewhere directly behind the sternum. A few weeks later, a young father informed me that after his family had just finished a particularly spiritual family home evening, his eight-year-old son told him, "I think Brother Frazer was wrong. The Spirit makes me feel good right here," while pointing to his heart. Far be it from me to dispute the findings of a child, especially one who listened so attentively to my testimony at church. In any case, his conclusion is widespread enough to accept that the Holy Ghost witnesses to our hearts. However, though we feel the stirrings or burning of the Holy Ghost in our hearts, this does not mean that the heart is the center of our spiritual beings, a retainer for our memories, or where we make decisions.

Is the "Heart" Also Where We Store Love?

Complicating the metaphor even further, the human heart has also been associated with romantic love for centuries. Again, we should consider the numerous times we use the word *heart* in reference to our love for one another. For example, I love my wife with all my heart, though before our marriage, she did break my heart a couple of times. She is my sweetheart. We have heart-to-heart talks. We give each other heart-felt thanks. She is close to my heart.

If read literally, these sayings make no sense at all. If your sweetheart actually "breaks your heart," then you'll die. Only a heart surgeon should be allowed to truly "touch your heart." Again, the heart metaphor is very ingrained into our language and thought processes. We must realize that our beating heart does not contain our spirituality or our love for our families and friends—despite the heart-shaped cards we share with each other on Valentine's Day.

But now we have a problem. We have forced your spiritual self out of your beating heart and into your mind. We have evicted the emotions of love that you have for your sweetheart, children, and friends from the heart—also into the brain. As we all know, the brain is the place where we conduct logical deduction, store memories, and make decisions about how we will live our lives. Emotions, tenderness, and spirituality are kept in the same place as our data processing center. You use the same brain to communicate with God as you do to remember how to scrub toilets or change a baby's dirty diaper. The same place you keep your admittedly sappy love for your spouse is the same place you store your understanding of gospel topics. Fortunately, your brain is up to the task. But having such wildly different aspects of your life in such close proximity to each other does cause some problems, as we will soon consider.

ENDNOTES

1. George Sarton, *Ancient Science through the Golden Age of Greece* (New York City: Dover Publications, 1993), 537.
2. Carl Zimmer, *Soul Made Flesh* (New York City: Free Press, 2004), 13.
3. Patricia S. Churchland, *Touching a Nerve* (New York: W.W. Norton & Company, 2013), 15.
4. National Heart, Lung and Blood Institute, nhlbi.nih.gov/health-topics/how-heart-works.
5. Jonathan Haidt, *The Happiness Hypothesis* (New York City: Basic Books, 2006), 4.
6. Haidt, *The Happiness Hypothesis,* 13.

CHAPTER 8

The Consciousness Conundrum

Early philosophers and Church leaders noted that only human beings have consciousness, only humans have a soul, and neither one can be found in an autopsy of the body. A logical conclusion was that the two were actually the same thing. Many people still believe this today. But research on the brain and conscious mind indicate this is not possible. The soul is not the same thing as the conscious mind. But we must start with a definition, so let's explore what consciousness is.

While brain mapping and other research has made significant progress through history, the concept of consciousness has continued to defy definition. Does the word refer to self-awareness, introspection, a state of being, subjective experience, or simply that you are awake? Learned men have argued over the definition of consciousness for centuries. Edward O. Wilson, a well-known biologist and author, once stated, "Most of the history of philosophy consists of failed models of the mind. The field of discourse is strewn with the wreckage of theories of consciousness."[1]

Cognitive psychologist George Miller lamented in 1960, "Consciousness is a word worn smooth by a million tongues. . . . Maybe we should ban the word for a decade or two until we can develop more precise terms for the several uses which 'consciousness' now obscures."[2] Despite this admonition, the debate continues even today. But for our own purposes, we need to define consciousness, at least in its most general terms.

For clarity's sake, we should note that there are two definitions for the word *consciousness*. First, consciousness can mean that you are awake. If you are asleep or in a coma, then you have lost consciousness. The second, more complex definition of consciousness is that you recognize that you are an individual who is a part of the world around you. You can evaluate your environment and, by thought and action, change that environment. You can empathize and feel sympathy. You can think about how you think. With your conscious mind, you can make decisions about abstract issues such as morality, justice, and mercy.

By this definition, consciousness can be credited with most inventions. The Sumerians decided that writing was an improvement over trying to remember how many sacks of grain were shipped out on a given day. Thomas Edison thought that electricity might be able to provide more light than candles or lanterns. Henry Ford imagined the automobile could be a better mode of transportation than the horse and buggy. George Washington and the Founding Fathers envisioned a better form of government and founded the United States of America. These men had a high degree of consciousness of their world and how it might be changed for the better. Then they changed it.

Instinct versus Consciousness

Part of the unconscious mind includes the natural instincts with which we are born. Instincts are inborn behaviors that do not have to be learned but assist in our survival. Instincts might be considered the opposite of consciousness. They vary with species. A newborn foal can walk within a few minutes of birth and run shortly thereafter. Before their domestication, horses had to run to evade predators. To survive, colts had to develop the instinct and ability to run very early in life, unlike clumsy humans who take a year or more to learn to walk. Puppies can't see immediately after birth, but they have the instinct to seek to suckle, and their mother has the instinct to let them do it. Man has bred heightened instincts into his domesticated animals as well. My border collie Gracie has the instinct to herd anything that moves. This instinct was bred into her by sheep herders who only bred the best herders on their ranches. Herding became instinctual for the breed. It still exists in my dog that has never seen a sheep in her life.

Consciousness in Animals

There is no doubt that man far outstrips any other species in our level of consciousness and intelligence. But, perhaps by looking at consciousness in other species, we can better understand more about this wonderful ability we have.

The Consciousness Conundrum

As our example of a species that has no consciousness, let's look at the cockroach. As far as we know, a cockroach has no consciousness. The purpose of life for a cockroach is simply to survive. It spends its time seeking food, shelter, and a mate. Cockroaches don't appear to ever be introspective about what they do. As far as we know, a cockroach will never wonder if there is a better way of finding food or a better place to live. But that unconscious approach to life has been very successful for the cockroach. They can, after all, be found in nearly every climate around the world. Cockroaches have managed to survive every global extinction event and ice age that earth has thrown at them for 280 million years. So one can argue, is consciousness all that necessary for a species to survive? Apparently not, because the cockroach has done just fine without it.

Consciousness appears to increase with intelligence. As a species becomes smarter, each individual becomes more aware of itself and its environment. Consciousness dawns slowly with the evolution of a species. Dogs appear to have what might be called a glimmer of consciousness. Returning to my border collie, I have watched Gracie try multiple approaches to solve problems. If her ball goes under a couch, she will try to get it from all sides and even corners. If that approach is unsuccessful, she stops and looks directly at me for help. She looks at the couch, then at me, back and forth until I understand her. Many will call this learned behavior, and I would agree with them. But dogs have the intelligence to evaluate a problem, be aware of the fact their solution is not working, and make adjustments. Thus they seem to have a glimmer of consciousness. As recounted by one researcher, "So, are other animals conscious? Science currently has no meaningful way to answer that question—but I offer two intuitions. First, consciousness is probably not an all-or-nothing quality, but comes in degrees. Second, I suggest that an animal's degree of consciousness will parallel its intellectual flexibility."[3]

Humans are of the primate family, which have enjoyed the most extensive evolution of the mind. Primates can understand numerous words. The most famous conversant non-human primate was Koko, a mountain gorilla who passed away in June 2018. Koko learned sign language and had a vocabulary of 1,000 words. Koko had a pet kitten, with which she was pictured on the cover of *National Geographic*. Koko showed that great apes are capable of loving, grieving, and reasoning about their world.

Likewise, chimpanzees have the beginnings of consciousness. Chimps are tool users, an ability which has long been recognized as an indicator of intelligence. They will mold a leaf to use as a drinking cup or use a long twig to fish out tasty termites from their mounds. Chimps are conscious of the fact that using a tool is a better option than not using it. Thus they exhibit another, slightly more advanced, level of consciousness.

The Conscious Minds of Pre-Adamites

Finally, we must consider the consciousness of pre-Adamites. Archeologists and historians have proven that numerous societies of men existed well before the time of Adam (about 4000 BC). From archeological digs, we find that different prehistoric branches of mankind left evidence of developing consciousness. *Homo erectus*, one of our earliest ancestors, lived from 1.8 million to 1 million years ago.[4] Erectus constructed dwellings for themselves and made tools such as bowls and spears out of wood. So their minds developed the ability of abstract thought—they imagined the object they wanted to make and then went on to create it. *Erectus* used his newly developed consciousness to make choices. More than any other change, this accomplishment introduced him into the community of mankind.[5]

Homo Neanderthal arose in Europe about 200,000 years ago, became quite widespread throughout the continent, and then became extinct 25,000 years ago. Neanderthals can be considered very distant cousins who split off from our evolutionary tree to form a branch of their own.[6] They had bigger brains than their predecessor species, about the same size as ours today. Neanderthals built more extensive shelters, made better tools, and lived in communities. They wore skins of animals as clothes and adorned themselves with jewelry. They buried their dead, though apparently more for practical reasons than religious belief. They had basic communication skills and may have had language. Evidence of such advancements indicates the gradual growth of consciousness within their thinking.[7]

Homo sapiens appeared about 140,000 years ago in Africa. About 40,000 years ago, *Sapiens* immigrated into the Near East, Asia, and Europe. By about 25,000 years ago, men were drawing, painting, and engraving pictures of animals on cave walls in France and Spain, a definitive sign of developing consciousness. Growing populations required that *Sapiens* change from hunter-gatherers to farmers who raised crops and domesticated animals. The oldest cultivated plants appeared in about 10,000 BC as agriculture started in Asia Minor and moved west.[8]

The Consciousness Conundrum

Evidence of the keeping of sheep, pigs, and cattle appeared in about 9,000 BC in northern Iraq.[9] By 5000 BC, communities began to look much like agrarian societies of today. Languages developed and with them the ability to teach new generations.

As one noted historian surmised, "By the end of prehistory, the human story is increasingly one of choice. Human beings are making more and more decisions to act and adapt in certain ways to meet their problems and to develop certain ways of doing things, to utilize certain materials or skills."[9]

These developments indicate the successful evolution of a well-formed conscious mind—and they all happened long before the birth of Adam. The Old Testament tells us that Adam was the first man who was given custody of a spirit child of our Heavenly Father. If you do the math, you can calculate that this happened around 4000 BC. At that time, about 7,000,000 people lived on the earth,[10] and they had all developed definitive traits of consciousness.

The timing worked out this way because both our *Sapiens* bodies and brains had to evolve enough to be worthy and capable of housing the spirit children of our Heavenly Father. Our bodies had to evolve to walk upright and develop in form and function. But our brains took the longest to evolve. Intelligence, improved memory, social capability, and consciousness all had to develop. After all, we know we were sent to this earth to make choices. We have a physical brain and a consciousness capable of making such decisions. We were given the right tools—body and brain—to accomplish our earthly tasks. Consciousness had to evolve in human beings long before Adam and Eve received their spirits. Thus, consciousness cannot be equated with our mortal spirits or souls. The timing simply does not work.

Thoughts Are Electrical Signals

Ancient Greek philosophers like Aristotle proposed that the physical brain was simply the hardware used by our spirit to express its thoughts and emotions. Many people still believe this today. But thoughts are not spiritual. Thoughts are mostly electrical.

In 1924, a German physiologist named Hans Berger recorded the first human electroencephalogram (EEG) by placing electrodes along a patient's head and using a sensitive voltmeter to measure the electrical signals caused by his firing neurons. He noticed that these electrical

73

signals, or "brain waves," varied in magnitude and frequency and could be charted. Different frequency brain waves predominate depending on the state of the person being monitored. The lowest frequency delta waves occur during sleep, as might be predicted. Theta waves are also associated with sleep and deep relaxation. Beta waves occur during active thought and problem solving. Gamma waves occur when we use our reasoning and planning functions.

As discussed in the chapter on the brain, our mind is filled with neurons that communicate through micro pulses of electric energy, initiated by separating oppositely charged ions across their membranes and then releasing them. As it turns out, we have a staggering number of neurons, giving our brains the capacity to hold many thousands of memories.

Colin McEvedy and Richard Jones, authors of *Atlas of World Population History*, wrote, "In the most fundamental sense, what the brain is—and thus who we are as conscious beings—is, in fact, defined by a sprawling network of 100 billion neurons with at least 100 trillion connecting points, or synapses."[11]

Your brain communicates with your body through electrical signals. Your nervous system uses electrical signals from the brain to move your limbs, talk, and blink. The senses of your body sends electrical signals back to the brain to tell it what is going on in the outside world. So it is rather consistent that your brain uses electrical signals to communicate with itself as well.[12]

With this model, a thought can now be defined as a particular pattern of firing and resting neurons. One could compare a thought or memory with a computer screen displaying a photo of, say, a goat. Certain pixels of the screen are illuminated, while others are dark. You look at that combination of illuminated and dark pixels and recognize it as a picture of a goat. In a similar way, your conscious mind looks at the firing and silent neurons in your brain and recognizes patterns that represent a particular memory, thought, or emotion. Some patterns may identify a certain smell your nose has picked up. Another pattern may communicate that your stomach is signaling some distress. Memories will be accessed from another part of your mind and displayed with firing and silent neurons for the conscious mind to consider. Since we have billions of neurons, we can generate billions of different patterns.

From data from EEGs and other brain scanning instruments, medical researchers have developed models that use electrical and chemical signals in the brain to reflect our thoughts, memories, and emotions. Thoughts are not spiritual or ethereal in nature. But your consciousness is still one of the greater mysteries and blessings of earth life. You are aware of yourself as an individual. You are conscious of your environment, the beauty that surrounds you, and of the people you love. Your conscious mind can recognize problems and work out solutions to them. You can read books and watch videos for either entertainment or education. Beyond these, hopefully you are conscious of your blessings and recognize their value in your life.

In conclusion, your conscious mind has been given control of your spirit body for its time on earth. I hope your mind understands that great responsibility and knows it has the capabilities to succeed. Your subconscious mind is there to help manage the many tasks needed every minute of every day to keep you alive and functioning. Your emotions and memories are designed to help you function as well. In the next chapter, we will discuss yet another entity that resides in your mind—your body's spirit.

ENDNOTES

1. Edward O. Wilson, *The Social Conquest of Earth* (New York City, W.W. Norton & Company, 2012), 9.
2. Gazzaniga, *The Consciousness Instinct*, 63–64.
3. Eagleman, *Incognito*, 143.
4. Thom Holmes, *Early Humans* (New York City: Infobase Publishing, 2009) 55.
5. Zimmer, *Soul Made Flesh*, 31.
6. J.M. Roberts, *A Short History of the World* (Oxford: Oxford University Press, 1993), 9–11.
7. Holmes, *Early Humans*, 79.
8. Ibid., 90
9. Ibid., 110–111
10. Roberts, *A Short History of the World,* 23–34.
11. Colin McEvedy and Richard Jones, *Atlas of World Population History,* (Middlesex England: Penguin Books, 1978), 344.
12. Max Bertolero and Danielle S. Bassett, "How Matter Becomes Mind," *Scientific American*, July 2019, Vol. 321 #1, 28.

CHAPTER 9

The Soul and the Spirit

Now that we have reviewed a small part of the complexity of our brains and consciousness, it is time to consider where your mind meets your spirit. What exactly is your soul, and where in your body does it reside? Is your soul the same thing as your spirit? How does our soul intersect with your body? Do the two communicate? These questions have been asked by philosophers, Church leaders, and physicians for centuries. There is a great deal of misinformation (available in hundreds of websites) about our spirits. Can a spirit haunt a spooky mansion? Can spirits communicate with us from the afterlife?

Before we launch into a review of the spiritual elements of our bodies, we need to realize that we know almost nothing about the spiritual worlds or spirit matter. We have we been taught almost nothing about premortal life or the spirit world. My only conclusion is that the Lord wants us to stay focused on this earth life, not the one before or the one after. How does our spirit travel? Can it eat or sleep? Is the spirit world a paradise or a prison? (See Luke 23:43, 1 Peter 3:19.) We know so little. Maybe the nature of our spiritual body and spiritual existence are so complex and foreign to us that the Lord decided to not even try to explain it. We may need a couple of afterlife classes (Spiritual Matter 101 & Introduction to Spirit Worlds 202) before we can really start to understand the spirit. We have very little information, but we do have the following oft-quoted revealed teaching by Joseph Smith: "There is no such thing as immaterial matter. All spirit is matter, but it is more fine or pure, and can only be discerned by purer eyes; We cannot see it; but when our bodies are purified we shall see that it is all matter" (Doctrine & Covenants 131:7–8).

By the way, this quote has been the source of a great deal of discussion for several decades. Long after Joseph's explanation, astrophysicists also proposed the existence of invisible matter. Through various measurements too complex to explain here, astronomers and physicists have calculated the mass of all the matter in the universe. But when they tried to balance that mass and its expected gravity with the orbits of the stars in the galaxy and galaxies in the universe, they came across a problem. There was simply not enough matter to explain the orbits of our stars and galaxies. In fact, the normal matter we can see makes up less than 10 percent of the matter that has to exist. Astrophysicists call this "dark matter" because it exerts gravitational pull but is invisible to the eye and any other electromagnetic radiation.[1] The similarities between Joseph's description of spiritual matter and dark matter are quite remarkable. But at this point, without further data, we can only speculate if they are related in any way.

Soul and Spirit

The words *soul* and *spirit* have multiple definitions that need to be unraveled before a discussion can begin. We first find the word *soul* very early in the scriptures: "And the Lord God formed man of the dust of the ground, and breathed into his nostrils the breath of life; and man became a living soul" (Genesis 2:7).

From this verse we might conclude that the soul results from the pairing of the premortal spirit and the body. Scriptures throughout the Old Testament and others confirm this definition (see D&C 88:15). Its usage can be fairly easy to recognize. If the word *soul* can be easily replaced by the word *person*, then this definition is in effect. This "body and spirit" definition is considered the semi-official definition of "soul" in many religious circles. But that translation is problematic. Old Testament usage implies that the soul was life itself and, since the body made up half of that soul, it disappeared at death. After all, when a man dies, his soul (body and spirit) is disassembled. By the Old Testament definition, the soul no longer exists until the Resurrection. Even then, since the Resurrection provides a new body, one could argue that it is a new soul (see 2 Nephi 9:13).

Many religions have taught that each person has an incorporeal, spiritual essence inside them. But it was the philosophers of ancient Greece who actually developed this concept. In 350 BC, Aristotle wrote a great deal about the subject, his main work entitled *De anima* or "On the Soul." Aristotle believed the soul to be the animating part of our being, also

The Soul and the Spirit

called our essence. In his book, Aristotle reviewed the prevailing theories about the soul and made his own comments and observations on those conjectures. He believed that the soul was a "subtle kind of body" overlaid on our physical body. This definition is actually very close to what many people still believe today. As Aristotle explained, "For if the soul is present throughout the whole percipient body, there must, if the soul be a kind of body, be two bodies in the same place."[2]

Aristotle spent a good deal of his writings speculating on the elements that made up the spirit body of the soul. One must remember that in 350 BC the Bible was essentially a history and code of ethics practiced by a strange people called Israel somewhere in the Middle East. Revelation about the spirit would not come for several centuries. Aristotle and the ancient Greeks could only use their powers of observation to realize that mankind was similar to, yet different from, other species. To differentiate plants, animals, higher animals, and man, Aristotle wrote, "All living beings have a nutritive soul (a soul that guides their nutrition and their material life); in addition, all animals have a sentient soul, which enables them to feel; in addition, some higher animals have an appetitive and locomotive soul; in addition, men have a rational soul."[3]

There is a startling logic to these ancient conclusions. Even the simplest organisms, plants, will seek out nutrition both from sunlight and through their root systems. Thus they have nutritive souls. Animals have a nervous system and a brain; thus they have 'sentient' souls on top of their nutritive souls. Higher animals have even more advanced souls that have appetites beyond nutrition and will travel long distances to meet those needs. Men have the most advanced souls, which include all the parts mentioned above plus a rational soul. Aristotle did not try to differentiate the soul from the psyche or mind. Spirit, soul, and mind were all considered the same thing in ancient Greece.[3]

The writings of Church leaders are, of course, affected by the definitions and beliefs that exist in their societies during their lifetimes. By the time of the New Testament, the definition of "soul" had changed to mean only the spiritual part of our beings. This is the part of you that will continue past death. Your soul is your spirit. Only with that definition do the following scriptures make sense.

> And fear not them which kill the body, but are not able to kill the soul: but rather fear him which is able to destroy both soul and body in hell. (Matthew 10:28)

> For what is a man profited, if he shall gain the whole world, and lose his own soul? Or what shall a man give in exchange for his soul? (Matthew 16:26)

> For the things which some men esteem to be of great worth, both to the body and soul, others set at naught and trample under their feet. (1 Nephi 19:7)

By the early fifth century, St. Augustine taught that the soul was a "rider" in the body. The soul was actually the true person, simply using the body as a vehicle and then vacating it upon death.[4] Debate on the subject continued throughout the Middle Ages. By the early 1500s, the Catholic Church declared that the soul was immortal and called upon all philosophers and teachers of religion to support that doctrine. Much of the debate revolved around the respective roles of the brain and spirit. Using a modern analogy, was the brain just the hardware of the biological computer in your head? Was the spirit the software that actually controlled the body? Or did the spirit take a more passive role, influencing the brain when possible, but not making any of its decisions? These questions are still being debated today.

Since the days of the New Testament, philosophers and medical practitioners have examined the human body and brain in a search for the mortal soul. They never found it, of course. But their theories and conclusions have survived for centuries. Perhaps a short review of the thoughts of a couple of these learned men will help us understand where many of our beliefs about the soul originated. Please forgive this deep dive into the teachings of long-dead philosophers, but to clarify our murky understandings of the soul/spirit, a little bit of history is required.

Rene Descartes and John Locke

Rene Descartes was a French philosopher born in 1596 who had a great influence on doctrine of the soul. Descartes was a mathematician and a scientist who knew that the body was a complex machine. Muscles, tendons, bones, joints, and organs all operated in concert to allow us to eat, breathe, walk, and live our physical lives. However, Descartes recognized that our thoughts, emotions, and memories were all non-physical and non-material. They only exist in our minds and could not be found in autopsies. Descartes concluded that the mind or soul that held those non-material thoughts had to be non-material as well. This theory, that the body was physical matter and the spirit and thoughts were non-material, came to be known as "mind/body dualism" and is still the belief of many people today.

Descartes was a devout Catholic.[5] He believed in the existence of the soul and believed that it resided somewhere in the head. But he came to doubt that the soul was the only active force in the body. Descartes noted that many actions, such as coughing, blinking, yawning, waking, and breathing, don't require thought or decisions. Descartes essentially figured out the presence of a subconscious mind. But he could not fit this discovery into his model that the mind and the soul were the same thing. How could part of your soul be subconscious, and for what purpose? How did the immaterial soul interact with the material body? Descartes finally came to the conclusion that unconscious acts were accomplished by the automatic responses of the body and that conscious decisions were made by the soul.

In his writings on the subject, Descartes introduced the word *conscious* to the world. Descartes defined consciousness to mean "the knowledge we have of what is passing in our minds."[6] But he knew his mind could be tricked, and he began to doubt all aspects of his reality. Descartes could doubt a lot about this world—including his memories and even what his own senses told him about his environment. But he could not doubt he was thinking. His consciousness of his own thoughts defined the one thing he knew to be true. His conclusion, "I think, therefore I am," is a saying that is still used today to denote the uniqueness of our consciousness and thought.

John Locke was an English philosopher born in 1632. Locke dabbled in medicine enough to form his own arguments about the mind and soul. Locke agreed with the standard definition that "consciousness is the perception of what passes in a Man's own mind."[7] But Locke disagreed with the teaching that that the mind and the soul were the same thing. His logic was based on the fact that when we sleep we are no longer aware of our surroundings or our thoughts. We lose consciousness during our sleep. But we do not lose our soul when we sleep. Thus the conscious mind and the soul had to be different.

Modern-Day Understandings

In the latter half of the 1800s, science started to break away from its agreement with religion that the soul or mind could be immaterial (spiritual). However the brain worked in creating and storing thoughts, memories, and emotions, it had to be explicable by brain chemistry and biology. Science would no longer tolerate proposals that the mind was spiritual, mystical, or built of elements not found in the periodic table.

In 1859, Charles Darwin published *On the Origin of Species*. By the time he published *The Descent of Man* in 1871, his theories about evolution by natural selection were well accepted by his peers and much of the general public. Opinion shifted further toward the belief that the human mind had simply evolved further than the minds of animals. It was recognized that a subconscious mind keeps the body alive and takes on those chores we can do without thinking about them. Researchers also became aware of a *pre*conscious mind that contains our memories and can be accessed by the conscious mind when we need to remember something.

Many years have passed since the conclusions of Aristotle, Descartes, and Locke. These men had no information about neurons, electrical brain waves, or brain imaging. Given their lack of data, they were mistaken in their conclusions that thoughts had to be initiated and powered by the human spirit. Today, we know that chemical and bioelectrical signals are the sources of our thoughts and emotions. Just like our arm moves when we command it, our brain pulls up memories and thoughts as we request them. The conclusions about the function of the brain fit the results of hundreds of medical studies on the subject. Though we know that the spirit does not play a starring role in your thought processes, it *is* present in your mind and influences it when it can.

Spirit vs. Spirit

Before moving forward with our discussion about the soul and the spirit, a distinction needs to be made. The Spirit (capital "S") as we find in the scriptures refers to the Holy Ghost, the Holy Spirit, or the Spirit of God. The Holy Spirit is the third member of the Godhead. He is often depicted as God's messenger who communicates both spiritual truth and confirmation of what God would have us do. Because He is a member of the Godhead, the Holy Ghost's name is always capitalized.

When the scriptures wish to refer to your individual spirit, the word always begins with a lowercase "s." This usage is consistent throughout the scriptures. Secondly, the words *soul* and *spirit* are often used interchangeably throughout the standard works (see Alma 40). In effect, the two words refer to the same spiritual entity, and there is no need to differentiate them. But *soul* can also mean a type of music and has changed definitions throughout the scriptures. Since the word *spirit* does not have as many definitions as does *soul*, we will use it preferentially in our discussion.

The Premortal Spirit

The third, less-used definition of the word *soul* is "premortal spirit." Another scripture (again using the words *soul* and *spirit* interchangeably) explains a bit about these spirits: "And God saw these *souls* that they were good, and he stood in the midst of them, and he said: These I will make my rulers; for he stood among those that were *spirits*, and he saw that they were good; and he said unto me: Abraham, thou art one of them; thou wast chosen before thou wast born" (Abraham 3:23; italics added).

For clarity's sake, in our discussion, we will use the term "premortal spirit" to denote the untainted spirit that lived in the premortal world and then came to earth to occupy your physical body.

With the definition presented in the New Testament, the spirit is a continuing, eternal entity. Your premortal, mortal, postmortal, and resurrected spirits are all the same spiritual being. However, since you have new experiences and learn with each passing day, your spirit is constantly changing. From the time you were old enough to form memories of earth life, your premortal spirit did not really exist anymore. It is now a part of your mortal soul (and we don't even know how big a part). The memories, experiences, and decisions of your mortal life have been added to those of your premortal life to become the spirit you have today. Just like a sixty–year-old grandfather has become a different person than the ten–year-old child he once was, your mortal spirit is now radically different from the spirit that once lived in the premortal world.

Your spirit is made up of all the memories, impressions, personality, and character that you developed both in the premortal world (as a premortal spirit) and now on earth. Once you die, your spirit will flee your body. We will refer to this new spiritual manifestation of yourself as the postmortal spirit. Last, of course, will come your resurrection and the creation of your resurrected body and spirit.

So, we must ask, with the debate on the existence and nature of the spirit/soul over the centuries, what do we know about it today? The scriptures can give us a general description:

- Your soul is immortal (Helaman 3:30).
- Your spirit retains memories. If your spirit did not retain our memories of the premortal world, you would not need a veil in place to block your memories of it. Since your brain will decompose, your spirit will also need to retain your memories of earth life, at least until the Resurrection (Alma 34:34).
- The Holy Ghost bears witness to your spirit (Romans 8:16).
- Spirits can make decisions, as some chose to follow Satan in premortal world (D&C 29:36).
- Your soul belongs to you, but it can be lost by you as well (D&C 101:38).
- Your spirit can be taught, as demonstrated when the Savior taught those in spirit prison (1 Peter 3:19).
- Our postmortal spirits will miss their bodies while they await the Resurrection (D&C 45:17, D&C 138:15–18).
- Your soul can be led to destruction and hell by Satan (D&C 10:22), or your soul can be saved and taken to rest in the kingdom of our Heavenly Father (D&C 16:6).
- These next two characteristics are somewhat less defensible. The only scriptural example of a visible, speaking spirit is of the Savior prior to His birth. The conclusion that any spirit can do the same thing is questionable at best.
- Your spirit can be made visible (Ether 3:6–16), but it is rare (Ether 3:15).
- Your spirit can speak (Ether 3:13, 3 Nephi 1:13).

Can I Lose My Soul?

There are multiple fates for your soul. According to the scriptures, you can lose your soul or see it killed or destroyed. You can even exchange your soul.

> And fear not them which kill the body, but are not able to kill the soul: but rather fear him which is able to destroy both soul and body in hell. (Matthew 10:28)

> And I will say to my soul, Soul, thou hast much goods laid up for many years; take thine ease, eat, drink, and be merry. But God said unto him, Thou fool, this night thy soul shall be required of thee: then whose shall those things be, which thou hast provided? (Luke 12:19–20)

The Soul and the Spirit

> For what is a man profited, if he shall gain the whole world, and lose his own soul? or what shall a man give in exchange for his soul? (Matt 16:26)

Once again, we run into the poetic wording so often used to describe the spiritual side of our lives. To put your mind to rest, your soul cannot be both immortal and destroyed or killed. Only your eternal progression can be destroyed, and only your chance to obtain the celestial kingdom can be killed. The phrase "thy soul shall be required of thee" is an interesting way of saying "you will die." The phrase "lose your soul" is an even more thought-provoking way of saying "you will fail to attain the celestial kingdom." The word *soul* is often used to convey a number of deep concepts regarding your future should you choose a more wealth-focused life.

But I still rather like the wording that you can exchange your soul. As you just read, Matthew 16:26 asks, "What shall a man give in exchange for his soul?" You mean you can, as the saying goes, actually "sell your soul to the devil"? There have been numerous stories (*Faust*), movies (*Ghost Rider, Bedazzled, Little Mermaid*) and songs ("The Devil Went Down to Georgia") based on the idea that it is possible to make an agreement with Satan or one of his agents. If Satan gives you the life you want to lead on earth, you agree to live in hell after you die. Though the stories and movies about making a deal with the devil are fictional, the basic concept is certainly true. Many people live their lives with no thought of showing appreciation for their blessings or seeking out a spiritual side of life. They truly are trading their souls, or more accurately the opportunity to live in the celestial kingdom, for earthly pleasure.

In reading these scriptures about the soul, one thing becomes apparent. Your conscious mind will make its choices. It can choose to be carnally minded and follow the lusts and temptations of the flesh, or it can be spiritually minded and respond to the promptings and teachings of the Holy Ghost. Both paths are open to you. Those choices will determine if you lose your soul or save it.

The Postmortal Spirit

Once you die, you become a postmortal spirit. We may experience some déjà vu from our life in the premortal world, but being without a body again will probably seem very strange. As explained by Alma, "Now, concerning the state of the *soul* between death and the resurrection—Behold, it has been made known unto me by an angel, that the *spirits* of all men, as soon as they are departed from this mortal body, yea, the *spirits* of all men, whether they be good or evil, are taken home to that God who gave them life" (Alma 40:11; italics added).

Once the body dies, the soul may now go to a place called paradise or spirit prison. These two names are both found in the New Testament as names for the same place. But they certainly bring up different images in the mind. We know that the Savior informed the two robbers crucified beside Him that they were bound for paradise that very day (see Luke 23:43). But Peter calls the same place a "prison" in 1 Peter 3:19. We know it is a place where we will await our resurrection, but not much more. Wherever it is, during our wait in the spirit world, the spirit needs to securely hold all our memories, experiences, character, opinions, loves, and personality.

The Resurrected Spirit

Though the soul matures, it continues on. When you die, your body will immediately start to decompose. Your spirit, however, will move on. In the Book of Mormon, Amulek explains this principle: "For that same spirit which doth possess your bodies at the time that ye go out of this life, that same spirit will have power to possess your body in that eternal world" (Alma 34:34).

This continuity of our spirits is necessary for us to be resurrected and judged for our actions. The spirit you have when you die is the same one with which you will be resurrected. The scriptures take great pains to reassure us that the resurrection will restore everything about us to its original condition.

> And now behold, is the meaning of the word restoration to take a thing of a natural state and place it in an unnatural state, or to place it in a state opposite to its nature? O, my son, this is not the case; but the meaning of the word restoration is to bring back again evil for evil, or carnal for carnal, or devilish for devilish—good for that which is good; righteous for that which is righteous; just for that which is just; merciful for that which is merciful. (Alma 41:12–13)

> Their sleeping dust was to be restored unto its perfect frame, bone to his bone, and the sinews and the flesh upon them, the spirit and the body to be united never again to be divided, that they might receive a fulness of joy. (D&C 138:17)

The soul shall be restored to the body, and the body to the soul; yea, and every limb and joint shall be restored to its body; yea, even a hair of the head shall not be lost; but all things shall be restored to their proper and perfect frame. (Alma 40:23)

Last, it is the responsibility of your spirit to be the non-physical repository of your memories, personality, and characteristics. When you pass away, your physical brain will decompose, so memories and personality must be stored within your spirit. For the perfect restorations discussed in these scriptures, a very accurate record of the righteousness and body frame (including limbs, joints, and even hair) will need to be kept. For this function, you can picture your spirit as being a spiritual, high-capacity "hard drive" that records your memories, emotions, and actions. When the resurrection takes place, this information stored in our souls will be used to restore us, both body and mind, to our "proper and perfect frame." When the time comes, that information will be downloaded into your resurrected body. The time you spend on your education on earth will not be wasted. You get to take it with you. In the Doctrine and Covenants we learn, "Whatever principle of intelligence we attain unto in this life, it will rise with us in the resurrection. And if a person gains more knowledge and intelligence in this life through his diligence and obedience than another, he will have so much the advantage in the world to come" (D&C 130:18—19).

Proofs of the Spirit World That Aren't

Many faiths believe that each of us has a spiritual self that lives on in a spirit world after our physical death. Though life after death and a spirit world are obviously matters of faith, many people want to prove their beliefs to themselves and to others before they die. Countless books have been written about how the spiritual world interacts with our physical world. Dreams, hypnosis, near-death experiences, drug-induced visions, Ouija boards, and séances all have been used as anecdotal evidence that the spirit world is real and that loved ones can communicate with us from there. However, if you look closely at these mystical experiences, most of them can actually be explained as partially unconscious minds trying to make sense of its surroundings.

Hypnosis

Mistaking mental states for spiritual experience has occurred for centuries. Emanuel Swedenborg (1688—1772) was a scientist in Sweden who published works on mathematics, chemistry, psychology, and anatomy. Later in life, he dedicated himself to exploring and writing about the realm of spirits and angels that he accessed using his own meditative trance.[8]

Hypnosis is the act of putting a person into a partially unconscious, relaxed, and highly suggestible state or trance. The hypnotized person is neither asleep nor fully awake, but somewhere in between. Self-hypnosis is not rare; you do it every time you zone out. If you stare at something, without focusing on it, relax, and let your mind wander or go blank, you are under a form of hypnosis. Being hypnotized generally means listening to the hypnotist's voice, allowing yourself to fall into a trance, and then following his instructions.

When starting a show, a hypnotist will often attempt to hypnotize everyone in the audience. He then pulls people from the audience who show signs of being mesmerized. Some minds can be hypnotized more easily than others. There are, in fact, over a dozen "Hypnotic Susceptibility Scales" available to determine a person's receptiveness to hypnosis.

Hypnosis has been marketed as a way for an individual to discover past lives that they had lived before their present incarnation. The theory is that the conscious mind is asleep, so the spiritual mind (that remembers its past lives) can recount its history. There is no way to check a recounting of course. Remember that a hypnotized person is in a very suggestible state. If asked to recount past lives, the mesmerized person will do their best to accommodate the request, even if it means letting their imagination run wild and making up a history.

Hypnotherapy can be used to treat mental anxiety, phobias, and pain management. It provides a unique access to the mind. Being in a suggestive state, the patient is often more open to directions and counseling by the therapist. Hypnosis has its place in the medical and mental health fields, but it is not a gateway to communication with deceased spirits.

Dreams

When you sleep, your conscious mind enters a reduced state of consciousness. Your brain is still monitoring your senses, which explains why

The Soul and the Spirit

a loud noise or someone shaking you will wake you up. But brain scans during sleep still show a lot of activity there. It has been proposed that memories of the day are being processed and stored in the correct areas of your brain. Although we are still unsure about the purpose of this nighttime brain activity, we know that dreams can result from it. For some people, those dreams are vivid, impactful, and easily remembered in the morning. Others can rarely remember their dreams at all.

Dreams can have a certain "dream-like" feel to them, which is depicted in movies by background clouds and mists that extend a foot or two off the floor. This dream-like state rather coincides with our mental picture of heaven or the spirit world, so many people have speculated that the two are linked. Thus, the theory goes, our dreams can be avenues through which our dead loved ones can communicate with us. For those who have had vivid dreams of such conversations, it may be hard to believe otherwise. There are numerous scriptures in which the Lord reveals His will through dreams. However, those dreams are always directed to His prophets, and the Lord is almost always speaking, not a dead ancestor. So, there is no scriptural proof that the dream state gives us insight into the spiritual realm or the opportunity to talk to an ancestor. It is revealing to note that we are *not* encouraged by Church leaders to look for God's revelation in our dreams. We should, instead, look for revelation in our prayers. Receiving revelation through prayer not only follows today's counsel, but it also allows you to receive God's instruction when your brain is awake and alert—not in a semi-conscious sleep.

Near-Death Experiences

In his 1978 bestseller *Life After Life*, Dr. Raymond Moody coined the term "near-death experiences." His book catalogued numerous accounts by people who had had near-death experiences. Patients who were coming out of a coma, anesthesia, or cardiac arrest told the narrative of what they witnessed while medical staff scrambled to revive them. The book prompted several research studies of the phenomenon. One of those researchers wrote in his own book that the most common near-death experience included an altered sense of being, a separation from the body, and a journey through a tunnel to a spirit world where they might encounter deceased relatives, spirit guides, and sometime religious figures like Jesus or God.[9]

The spiritualist explanation of near-death experiences is that since the person is poised on death's door, they can see what is on the other side of the veil that separates earth life and the next one. Though it is not supported by the scriptures, such a theory cannot really be proven one way or the other. Those persons who have near-death visions are often very emotional about their experiences. While potentially interesting, we should not base our understanding of gospel doctrine on such events.

The medical explanation of near-death experiences is that when a patient is coming out of surgery or the midst of cardiac arrest, the brain is not in peak condition. Often, anesthesia has forced the brain into unconsciousness from which it is still recovering. Blood pressure often varies significantly, and the brain is receiving all kinds of emergency alert signals from affected parts of the body. The brain is desperately trying to make sense of what is going on. Swiss neurologist Olaf Blanke ran a number of experiments to simulate near-death experiences. He discovered that a region in the right tempoparietal junction, when impaired or electrically stimulated, causes an out-of-body sensation. This region of the brain lets you know your body's location relative to its environment. Are you lying down? Where is your right arm? By creating specific visual and touch signals to disorient the brain, Blanke could elicit an out-of-body experience in a normal, wide-awake brain.[10]

Certain drugs can also prompt out-of-body experiences. Ketamine is a controlled yet abused party drug. It belongs to a class of drugs known as "dissociative anesthetics," in that it causes a person to feel detached from reality. The user can feel so detached from their sensations and surroundings that they feel like they are floating outside their body. The fact that researchers can recreate near-death experiences through disorientation and drugs strongly indicates that there is a neurobiological explanation to near-death experiences.

As mentioned, many near-death experiences include a journey through a tunnel. As it turns out, tunnels are fairly common as one loses consciousness or recovers it. Once while giving blood at the local blood drive, I noticed that the edges of my vision started to darken. I was more than a little confused. I remember thinking how strange it was that I was seeing the far wall like it was at the end of a tunnel. When a nurse asked how I was doing, I described the effect. Fortunately, she immediately recognized this symptom of low blood pressure. My body was going into shock, quickly lowering my blood pressure to reduce blood loss in case I

The Soul and the Spirit

was bleeding to death. Immediately the nurse called for some help, had me lay back on the exam table, and removed the needle. After I had recovered, she gently suggested that I not give blood in the future.

It would be satisfying to be able to prove through dreams, hypnosis, or near-death experiences that a spirit world really does exist. But once again, we live in a world of faith. We are not meant to be able to prove that God or an afterlife exists with the results of a few studies. The mind can do some pretty strange things when we are hypnotized, asleep, or dying. However realistic, any visions we have while semi-conscious must be suspect and not taken to be a glimpse through the veil into the spirit world. Many Christians very badly want proof of an afterlife and to talk to loved ones who have passed away. But such proof is not to be had, not in this world at least.

ENDNOTES

1. Martin Rees, *Just Six Numbers* (New York City: Basic Books, 2000), 84.
2. Richard McKeon, ed. *Introduction to Aristotle* (New York City: Random House, 1947), 165.
3. Sarton, *Ancient Science through the Golden Age of Greece*, 533.
4. *Encyclopedia Britannica*, britannica.com/topic/soul-religion-and-philosophy.
5. Zimmer, *Soul Made Flesh*, 34–35.
6. Gazzaniga, *The Consciousness Instinct*, 27.
7. John Locke, *An Essay Concerning Human Understanding* (New York City: Oxford University Press, 1975), 115.
8. Neil Drury, *The New Age* (London: Thames & Hudson, 2004), 13.
9. Drury, *The New Age*, 182–192.
10. Dehaene, *Consciousness and the Brain*, 44–45.

CHAPTER 10

Being Conscious of your Conscience

We have determined that your premortal spirit, though it communicates with your mind, is not your mind. Much like the Holy Ghost gives you inspiration, your own spirit can be one of the voices in your head, trying to counsel you what to do. First, however, we need to find it or determine the following: What is the outward manifestation of your spirit? Which aspect of your personality reflects the desires and urgings of the spirit child of our Heavenly Father? Only one aspect of our make-up really reflects the type of behavior we might expect of a spirit—our conscience.

We have examined the definitions of several words whose meanings have changed over time. What is a conscience? In a quick survey of popular literature, there has been very little written about the conscience. However, there was one Disney movie that mentioned it.

In *Pinocchio*, a kindly old toymaker named Geppetto constructs a little boy puppet and names him Pinocchio. Geppetto had longed for a child of his own, so a magical Blue Fairy animates Pinocchio, giving him life. Apparently, Pinocchio has a working mind so he can walk and talk, but he has no sense of right and wrong. The Blue Fairy assigns a cricket named Jiminy to be Pinocchio's conscience. Jiminy is to keep Pinocchio from making poor, unrighteous choices. He is supposed to guide Pinocchio in his decisions on what is wrong and what is right. But Jiminy is only a cricket, after all, and Pinocchio ignores Jiminy's guidance at the encouragement of some poorly chosen peers. Pinocchio gets himself into dire, life-threatening trouble. But, since it is a Disney movie, Pinocchio finally listens to Jiminy (his conscience) and redeems himself in the end. Due to his acts of self-sacrifice and love, the Blue Fairy transforms Pinocchio from being a wooden puppet into a real boy of flesh and bones.

As we just discussed, when your *conscious* mind is fully functioning, you are aware of your surroundings, your emotions, and thoughts. If you lose consciousness, you lose that ability. However, your *conscience* is "the inner sense of what is right or wrong in one's conduct or motives, impelling one toward right action."[1] We sometimes refer to our conscience as the Light of Christ (Moroni 7:19, John 1:9) or a moral compass. Your conscience will be troubled if you do something illegal, rude, or insensitive. Conscientious people strive to be led by their conscience, being mindful and exemplary in everything they do and say. Though animals may have the beginnings of a conscious mind, they do not have a conscience, as explained many years ago by Elder Joseph Fielding Smith: "Animals do not have a conscience. They cannot sin and they cannot repent, for they have not knowledge of right and wrong."[2]

According to the Bible Dictionary, "We are born with a natural capacity to distinguish between right and wrong, due to the Light of Christ that is given to every person (D&C 84:44–53). We have a faculty by means of which we can pass judgment on our own conduct, either approving or condemning it."[3]

The word *conscience* is not found in the Old Testament, perhaps because the ancient definition of the soul did not allow a place for a conscience. In the New Testament, the conscience and the Light of Christ are mentioned numerous times. We know that every person starts with a conscience (see D&C 84:46), but its influence can be deadened through misuse (see Titus 1:15, Timothy 4:2). Generally, we seek to have a "conscience void of offense toward God and toward men" (Acts 24:16) or, in other words, a "pure conscience" (1 Timothy 3:9).

Our Spiritual Selves

In past chapters we have searched for evidence of your spirit in your heart, your consciousness, and your brain. One would think it might be easier to locate the spirit. But we live in a world of faith, and the spirit must stay hidden. When God provides someone a blessing, be it a medical miracle or finding lost car keys, that blessing must have a natural explanation. If an inexplicable but documented miracle ever occurs, then faith becomes unnecessary. So, God cannot be discovered by science. Thus, brain surgeons and physicians have never been able to find a mortal spirit via surgery, electroencephalograph, or magnetic resonance imaging. If they did, the world would be forced to accept the existence of God. Faith in God would be unnecessary after such a discovery.

Thus, the spirit cannot be a vital piece of the workings of the brain or it would have been discovered by now. The spirit must be outside of our thinking process and even beneath our consciousness of it. This may be disappointing to those who believe they interact with their spirit with every thought. The veil over your mind that blocks memories of the pre-mortal world must be thick enough to meet its purpose. A separation of the physical processes of our minds and the presence of a spirit must be maintained.

The dilemma in defining a functioning brain and a spiritual side is explained by David Eagleman, a brain scientist and author:

> The *you* that all your friends know and love cannot exist unless the transistors and screws of your brain are in place. If you don't believe this, step into any neurology ward in any hospital. Damage to even small parts of the brain can lead to the loss of shockingly specific abilities: the ability to name animals, or to hear music, or to manage risky behavior, or to distinguish colors, or to arbitrate simple decisions... All of this leads to a key question: do we possess a soul that is separate from our physical biology—or are we simply an enormously complex biological network that mechanically produces our hopes, aspirations, dreams, desires, humor, and passions?[4]

My answer to Eagleman is that we are both. We are "an enormously complex biological network" that mechanically produces our hopes, dreams, and passions. That network is found within the brain tissue. We also "possess a soul that is separate from our physical biology." Though its location remains unknown, it makes sense that the spirit can be found in the brain as well.

While some people may be uncomfortable with the term "conscience," it is accepted that most people have an inner sense of right and wrong. So, one must ask, "Where does our conscience come from?" There are actually three theories. If you are a *nativist*, you believe that we are born with moral knowledge. If you are an *empiricist*, you believe that children are blank slates at birth and learn moral knowledge from parents and peers. Finally, if you are a *rationalist*, you still believe babies are blank slates but that they reason out morality for themselves.[5]

A number of books have been written to determine if research supports one theory over the others. In his book *The Righteous Mind*, author

Jonathan Haidt reviews studies performed by behavioral researcher Elliot Turiel:

> His innovation was to tell children short stories about other kids who break rules and then give them a series of yes-or-no probe questions. For example, you tell a story about a child who goes to school wearing regular clothes, even though his school requires students to wear a uniform. . . . Turiel discovered that children *as young as five* usually say that the boy was wrong to break the rule, but that it would be okay if the teacher gave permission. . . . Children recognize that rules about clothing, food, and many other aspects of life are *social conventions*, which are arbitrary and changeable to some extent. . . . But young children don't treat all rules the same. In another short story, the same children were asked if it was wrong for a girl to push a boy off of a swing because she wants a turn. Nearly all the children said this not okay—even if the teacher said it was permitted. . . . Children recognize that rules that prevent harm are *moral rules*. . . . They seem to grasp early on that rules that prevent harm are special, important, unalterable, and universal.[5]

Very small children will often loudly declare that a parental decision or a playmate's action is "not fair." So a sense of justice seems to manifest itself early in life. Empiricists and rationalists believe that children are born as blank slates who learn from parents, friends, or their own observations about what is fair. But a significant argument against these theories is the simple question, "Is there *time* for small children to learn moral principles before they start to recognize what is fair?" Are young children with developing brains able to learn moral judgment as toddlers? Will young children have witnessed enough examples of "fair" and "unfair" to be able to judge that everyone should take turns with toys, share cookies 50/50, and not cut to the front of lines? This seems rather unlikely. While commuting to work, I have seen plenty of adults who do not seem to understand the principle of waiting their turn. Do these parents understand the concept well enough to teach it to their young children?

In any case, the theory that babies are born with a blank slate is a stretch of the imagination because small children seem to figure out concepts of justice and fairness so early in life. The only conclusion is that children are born with a basic understanding of right and wrong. Sadly, life experiences as toddlers will often modify their fledgling moral code. For example, a toddler may learn that physical strength *does* allow bigger kids to get their way more often. At first, their minds may object to this moral violation. But children are impressionable. If an unfair action is not halted and chastised, then the action becomes a fact of life and the child's understanding of life's moral code is modified.

If conscience cannot be attributed to a cultural education, there are only two possibilities for the origin of our conscience. Either your conscience comes written in your DNA (such as your repugnance to the smell of spoiled meat), or it comes as part of the package that is your spiritual self.

Is Your Conscience Written in Your DNA?

Could kindness, righteousness, empathy, and a sense of fairness have been written into our DNA over the millennia of the evolution of animals and man? The arguments for such a possibility are weak for several reasons.

"Survival of the fittest" is the mantra of evolution. Every insect, bird, reptile, and mammal has been given the assignment to pass on its individual genes to the next generation of its species. This means the animal must stay alive, so battles for food are inevitable. It means the individual must find a mate and have children. But fairness finds no place in survival of the fittest. The biggest lion of the pride does not stop eating a fresh kill so that the younger lions will have enough to eat. The largest hippopotamus in the river does not allow females from his harem to leave with smaller male hippos to start their own families. Animals will battle to the death for access to food and mates.

There is nothing fair or just about the law of the jungle. Is it fair that a leopard does the work of bringing down a gazelle and then has a pack of hyenas steal it away? Does it seem fair that only the largest, strongest caribou, elephant seal, lion, or gorilla in a group gets to mate and produce offspring? Or is it moral that a lion, once he has displaced the former alpha male of the pride, will often kill the cubs of his predecessor to cause the lionesses to be ready to breed sooner? Probably not, but neither nature nor evolution have ever claimed to be moral or fair. So, is it likely that evolution instilled in us the instinct to be fair or just, when it has demonstrated no such inclinations in millions of species over millions of years?

One may be tempted to think that the herding of mammals, flocking of birds, and schooling of fish is at least the start of unselfish cooperation. But no, even the motives behind these activities are selfish. Herds of bison and elephants stick together because they can cooperate in defending the herd from predators. Birds flock and fish school also for the protection a group gives to the individual. With more eyes looking out for hunters and more voices to cry out an alarm, a flock of birds is less likely to be surprised by a camouflaged predator or an attack from above. A school of fish can disorient an attacker by the sheer number of individual fish flashing by as they flee. The socialization of animals originated from selfish interests.

Our brain is the result of millions of years of evolution, developed under the rules of the survival of the fittest. It is believed that our rewards center developed as a way for the mind to encourage the body to do things that would ensure its survival. For example, we are given a dopamine burst when we eat high fat, high caloric foods—because we are now less likely to starve to death. We receive other such rewards when we find warmth and shelter from the cold. Any action that helps us survive and procreate children is rewarded. Brain researchers have been able to link many of our brain characteristics to abilities we evolved to better survive in the wild. Even love for our children is significantly based on our compulsion to propagate our DNA. Right after a woman bears a child, a flood of oxytocin, endorphins, prolactin, and other hormones are released and help her to bond with this new, cute, yet squalling baby. Most mammals have the same maternal instincts and will protect their young to the death.[6]

As animals form herds, flocks, schools, and gaggles, men have also formed communities. There is protection and safety in numbers. Humans can protect one another when they form groups, with the common goal of surviving attacks by other mammals or, much more likely, other humans. There are also advantages for groups in collecting food. Lions form prides, wolves form packs, and humans form hunting parties because it is easier to hunt and bring down large prey by working as a group. For many species, including our own, it appears that "survival of the fittest" also means survival of the most cooperative.

But there are other human characteristics that cannot be explained well by evolution. For example, compassion and charity are not characteristics that will help you survive the cold realities of life. If you give away your food to the hungry, what will happen to you in the next famine? If you give away your clothes, can you survive the upcoming winter? If you are merciful and do not slay your enemies when you have the chance, will you survive their future plots and attacks? Does altruism, the selfless concern for the well-being of others, have a place in our evolution?

Famed atheist Richard Dawkins wrote a book called *The Selfish Gene*. In it, Dawkins makes a case for the argument that evolution would *not* build into us traits such as charity, self-sacrifice, bravery, or sympathy. Granted, animals and humans have maternal and paternal instincts such that their own genes will be carried forward. But evolution does not build altruism and self-sacrifice into a species. As the title of the book suggests, genes and evolution are selfish. As Mr. Dawkins observes, "The commonest and most conspicuous acts of animal altruism are done by parents, especially mothers, towards their children. . . . But first I must deal with a particular erroneous explanation for altruism, because it is widely known, and even widely taught in schools. This explanation is based on the misconception . . . that living creatures evolve to do things 'for the good of the species or 'for the good of the group.'"[7]

Mr. Dawkins goes on to explain that evolution would eventually breed out altruism from a group of animals or humans. "Even in the group of altruists, there will almost certainly be a dissenting minority who refuse to make any sacrifice. If there is just one selfish rebel . . . then he, by definition is more likely than they are to survive and have children... Even while the group is going slowly and inexorably downhill, selfish individuals prosper in the short term at the expense of altruists."[8]

There is a great difference between the goals of our evolved bodies and our spirits. Your spirit cares about the welfare of others. The instincts of our bodies care only for the survival of you and your family. The British poet Alfred, Lord Tennyson expressed the difference between God's love and Nature's savagery in the following famous verse.

> Who trusted God was love indeed
> And love Creation's final law
> Tho' Nature, red in tooth and claw
> With ravine, shriek'd against his creed[9]

Indeed, the savagery of nature is a sharp contrast to God's love. Nature put demands on mankind, so evolution had to provide us with the physical build and mental capacity to survive them. There is no right and wrong in nature. There is no charity either. It is very unlikely that evolution would have written a conscience into your DNA.

Knowledge of Good and Evil

To better understand our spiritual sides, one more point needs to be made. With whatever knowledge he brought to the Garden and his new spirit, Adam was able to give names to all the animals and birds. He also insightfully recognized his responsibility to his wife. Nonetheless, Adam and Eve were both naked in front of their God and were not ashamed or uncomfortable about it (see Genesis 2:19–25). They were as little children, or, metaphorically speaking, their eyes were not yet open. The first couple then ate the fruit of the tree of knowledge of good and evil. With the Fall, Adam and Eve became mortal, could have children, and began to gain additional knowledge of good and evil. We do know that this knowledge included modesty. Immediately after partaking of the fruit, the first couple discovered their nakedness and made themselves aprons. We don't know what knowledge their premortal spirits brought with them, but it seems Adam and Eve's understandings had to be supplemented before they could leave the Garden.

Since then, of course, all of Adam and Eve's descendants have been born with their consciences intact as part of their spiritual selves. Tendencies toward fairness and charity are strengthened in our childhood, as our parents teach us how to act and treat others. We each have a conscience, nudging us to be righteous and kind. I have heard many people try to justify their rude, selfish, or dishonest actions with myriads of excuses. It seems they are desperately hoping others' acceptance of their poor choices will help quiet their consciences. It is a strange inner voice, as we might expect any spirit/mind interaction to be.

Laws of the Land

During his evolution and competition with other species, prehistoric man had to follow the same rules of survival as other animals. They learned that banding together helped them in their survival. Hunting and defense were more effective in groups. But socialization had its challenges as jealousies, competitiveness, and power struggles caused discord and even deaths within the camp. Rules of cooperation and socialization had to be established for societies to grow. Laws had to be established and enforced. Thus, rule-making began in prehistoric times and has gone on for millennia. We find rules about dealing with other people throughout the Old Testament. Interestingly, it seems mankind has always divided itself into groups, clans, and nations. Rules and rights of people within your group are different than the rules and expectations of those outside your group. For example, the Mosaic law differentiated how an Israelite dealt with other Israelites and how an Israelite dealt with peoples that were not of the twelve tribes (see Leviticus 25:39–46). The Constitution of the United States also includes rules of behavior expected within our government and society. It outlines rules, rights, and expectations of the citizens of our country. Non-citizens have other obligations and fewer rights. So, much of what we understand as fair and unfair since childhood must be detailed, written down, and enforced as adults. Such laws give power to our consciences to be able to enforce fairness and justice within our society. With such laws, we can hopefully become a civilized society. The alternative is to sink to the kill-or-be-killed rules of the wild.

In summary, there is no reason to conclude that our moral values are written into our DNA. Morality is not instinctual. Admirable traits like bravery, prompting a man to fight on the front lines of a battle, would only get him killed and his DNA eliminated from the gene pool. Like-wise, being charitable may make you popular for a while, but in lean times your generosity increases your chances of starvation. Doing the "right thing" has a different definition when you don't live in a modern civilization with an abundance of food and shelter. Basic instincts of the body are very different from the desires of the spirit.

The Desire to Worship

A second indicator of the presence of a spirit in each of us may be found in our desire as a people to worship gods. Every society discovered in the world has worshipped gods in some fashion. Some of these cultures were found in isolated locations of the world where missionaries had not yet ventured. How did religion begin independently in all corners of the earth? The ubiquitous nature of religion has been recognized by both those who promote religious observation and those who fight it.

James Talmage, author of *Jesus the Christ* and *Articles of Faith*, recognized, "Every nation, every tribe, every individual, yearns for some object of reverence. It is natural for man to worship; his soul is unsatisfied until he finds a deity."[10]

Talmage went on to say that even when societies of men fell into darkness and established idols and false deities, they demonstrated "man's hereditary passion for worship." The spirit in each of us prompts us to seek after God and worship Him. When the truth about Heavenly Father and Jesus Christ is not available to a society, its people will fabricate new gods around their own understanding of what deities should be like. They will invest these gods with powers and characteristics they believe gods should possess. Often, the nature and worship of these fabricated gods falls far outside of what we might expect of a religion, but societies reflect their own values in the gods they worship.

Evolutionists and atheists have also recognized that societies of men throughout the history of the world have developed religion. However, they refuse to attribute this urge to worship to a spirit within us. They must instead look to an evolutionary event that installed in us the desire to worship. As Sir Richard Dawkins states his case in his book *The God Delusion*, "Everybody has their own pet theory of where religion comes from and why all human cultures have it. . . . Knowing that we are products of Darwinian evolution, we should ask what pressure or pressures exerted by natural selection originally favoured the impulse to religion."[11]

Dawkins went on to examine different explanations of what drives humans to want to worship a god. He examined "group-selection" theory that states that evolution would favor more tight-knit groups of people, which religion could provide. But he also admitted that there were formidable objections to the theory and even he didn't support it. He suggested that religion is a by-product of obedience and other principles of religion that help keep children safe into adulthood. Although I am an advocate of evolutionary theory, it strains logic to credit natural selection for the desire to worship God. The simplest explanation of an inner desire to find and worship God is that we have a spirit within us which influences us towards religious worship.

Our Conscience—Your Spiritual Self

Being born with a conscience allows us to recognize right and wrong and thus gives us a foundation on which to build our spiritual beliefs and understanding. It also provides us a starting point of how to interact with other people, respect other people's possessions, and obey the laws of the land. Our consciences must learn and develop too. It is fascinating to watch young children interact, as they will be selfish one moment and charitable the next. When someone mentions their own conscience, it usually accompanies a declaration that theirs is clear or untainted. Paul said, "And herein do I exercise myself, to have always a conscience void of offence toward God, and toward men" (Acts 24:16). Joseph Smith restated Paul's sentiment as he traveled to Liberty Jail, knowing that this would be a fatal choice and he only had a few days of life remaining: "I am going like a lamb to the slaughter; but I am calm as a summer's morning; I have a conscience void of offense towards God, and towards all men" (D&C 135:4).

Being Conscious of Your Conscience

As with Paul and Joseph Smith, our consciences can be strong enough to cause us to do unpopular things in an unrighteous world. We should not think that the conscience is simply a Pollyanna-like voice that can be easily ignored. Conscience is more than that, as has been demonstrated in countless examples of heroism throughout history. Another important figure in religious history who bravely followed his conscience is Martin Luther, the founder of the Lutheran Church.

Martin Luther and His Conscience

In the year 1517, Martin Luther started down a path that led him to become the leader of the Protestant movement that swept throughout Germany. It all started when Luther strongly opposed the practice of the Catholic Church of selling indulgences (forgiveness of sins) and other such practices. He wrote a document that became known as the "Ninety-five Theses" or doctrines. Legend has it that he nailed this document to the door of the Catholic cathedral in Wittenberg, Germany. In any case the document was translated from Latin to German and circulated broadly. In 1521, Martin Luther was excommunicated from the church, but he kept on preaching and writing.

Shortly thereafter, Luther was commanded to appear for trial before Emperor Charles V in Worms, Germany. Luther was to appear before the emperor to defend himself of charges of heresy. Luther knew that this appearance could lead to his death, so he obtained a promise that he would be allowed safe passage to and from the trial. Still, after safe passage home, Luther knew that Charles V would probably have had him jailed or executed as a result of the judgment.

As the trial started, the titles of all of the books and treatises Martin Luther had ever written were read aloud. Referring to his publications, Luther was asked, "Will you recant?" In the end, Luther gave the following response: "Unless I am convinced by scripture and by plain reason . . . in those scriptures that I have presented, for my *conscience* is captive to the Word of God, I cannot and I will not recant anything, for *to go against conscience is neither right nor safe*. Here I stand; I can do no other. God help me, Amen."[12]

During his journey home, Luther's supporters staged a kidnapping, and he was secreted away into hiding. Edicts were sent out by the emperor that declared Luther a heretic and a fugitive of the empire. He and his allies were to be considered outlaws and lose their properties. His books

103

were burned. All of this occurred because Martin Luther refused to ignore his conscience. By his example, we might recognize that our conscience should be a powerful force in shaping our lives as well.

Conscience Reinforced

As parents, we should seek to reinforce our children's inborn sense of justice and fairness. We can ask questions like, "Is it fair to take your sister's cookie after you ate yours?" We all have a conscience, and we know our children do as well. As a parent, you can be certain that if your little son hedges about whether stealing a cookie was wrong, you can tilt your head and stare at him. Usually, he will break under the pressure and admit his wrongdoing. As parents, it is critically important to reinforce what your children's conscience tells them. We must continue to teach that "fair is fair," as the saying goes. The lessons must be taught. We baptize our children at the young age of eight years old because we believe they have learned the difference between right and wrong by that time. Yet, these children are beginning readers who have never taken a moral philosophy class. Fortunately, because of the head-start their spiritual consciences provide them, young children are soon able to judge fairness in a multitude of different situations. By the age of eight, they can begin to take responsibility for their judgments.

In summary, your conscience is the only aspect of your spiritual self that you can mentally examine and consider. If you want to better know your spiritual self, getting to know your conscience is a good place to start. Your conscience has two main functions. First, it is to encourage you to respect yourself—your mind and body. They are both gifts for your mortal probation, and you have a responsibility to care for them. Second, your conscience urges you to be fair, charitable, and respectful to your fellow man. As discussed, loving your family is partly driven partly by your DNA in an effort to propagate your genes. Caring for those outside of your family and community is driven by your conscience. Learning to recognize the voice of your own conscience is highly recommended. That inner voice can tell you how to distinguish right and wrong, even when logic fails.

Having defined the components of our brain and spirit, it is time to discuss their interaction with the outside world. Our brains and spirits have the courage and strength to fight against the world's temptations. But they also have weaknesses of which we must be aware. First our brains must deal with the worries and anxieties of everyday life. Such anxieties are very hard on the mind. If left unchecked, fear can destroy our own self-confidence to make good choices. We will discuss drugs and medications and their ability to get through the brain's internal security system to produce energy, euphoria, drunkenness, or addiction. We will discuss addiction to stimuli provided by video games, the internet, and social media that reward your brain for accomplishments in the virtual world. Having described and discussed aspects of our spirit, we now need to turn our attention back to the brain.

ENDNOTES

1. "Conscience," Dictionary.com
2. *Elder Joseph Fielding Smith Man: His Origin and Destiny* (Salt Lake City: Deseret Book, 1954) 204–205.
3. Bible Dictionary of The Church of Jesus Christ of Latter-day Saints
4. Eagleman, *Incognito*, 203.
5. Jonathan Haidt, *The Righteous Mind* (New York City: Vintage Books, 2012), 11–12.
6. Haidt, *The Righteous Mind*, 5–6.
7. Richard Dawkins, *The Selfish Gene—40th Anniversary Edition* (Oxford: Oxford University Press, 1989), 8.
8. Dawkins, *The Selfish Gene*, 10.
9. Alfred Lord Tennyson, "In Memoriam," poets.org/poem/memoriam-h-h
10. James E. Talmage, *Articles of Faith* (Salt Lake City: The Church of Jesus Christ of Latter-day Saints, 1970), 29.
11. Richard Dawkins, *The God Delusion* (New York City: Houghton Mifflin Company, 2006), 163.
12. Richard Marius, *Martin Luther* (Cambridge, Massachusetts: Harvard University Press, 1999).

CHAPTER 11

Worry, Anxiety, and Fear

According to Murphy's law, if something can go wrong, it will go wrong. This is a pretty pessimistic viewpoint on life, but most people will admit to often believing it. We tend to remember an event better if there is an intense emotion attached to it. Our brains also remember our negative emotions better than our positive ones. For example, when we are in a hurry, we remember the one red light and forget about the three green ones.[1] We remember the things that go wrong much better than the things that go right—which may explain why Murphy's law became a law in the first place. When our minds vividly remember the negatives in our lives, we may conclude that the world is out to hurt us or the ones we love. Focusing on the negatives, we may decide that only by steadfast diligence can we fight back the forces in the universe that combine against us. We worry and become anxious, trying to outguess and outmaneuver the next attack on our home and family.

Worry and anxiety are different. Worry comes from the rational, thinking side of your brain. On a positive note, a little worry can be good for you. In making plans or solving problems, your conscious brain must look for weaknesses in your solutions. Are your plans feasible? Are your resolutions logical? Worry helps you fine-tune your plans such that they are more workable and likely to succeed. A little worry prevents you from being indifferent to your assignments and responsibilities. However, too much worry takes the fun out of life. Whether the problem is that you are feeling a little congested or the world is under attack by a new virus, practiced worriers will dwell on their troubles. Habitual worriers can never enjoy their plans or accomplishments, because neither is ever perfect—and they must forever worry about those deficiencies.

Anxiety, in contrast, originates from the limbic system, or the emotional side of your brain. A highly anxious person is preoccupied by the what-ifs of life. What if my child is kidnapped? What if my husband loses his job? Neuroscientist Alex Kolb explained, "Anxiety and fear activate the same stress response in brain and body, but anxiety is different from fear. . . . Fear is a response to actual danger that is right here, right now, while anxiety is concern for events that only might happen... Put another way, fear comes from seeing a lion jump out of the grass and start running toward you. Anxiety comes from seeing the grass rustle and assuming that a lion is hiding there."[1]

Anxiety stems from natural processing by the brain. A little anxiety is beneficial, since figuring out the what-ifs in life can help you avoid tragic accidents. If you are stepping to the edge of a sheer cliff or driving your car while wrestling with your toddler in the back seat, asking a what-if question can be very valuable. But high anxiety is bad for you. High anxiety, like worry, is a negative emotion. It can put you into a fight-or-flight mode, causing high levels of adrenaline and stress hormones. Even before the coronavirus, anxiety has been on the rise for the past several decades. The best example of this rise can be found in parents.

Parental Anxiety

My childhood was very different from that of my young grandchildren. I remember biking all over my hometown. My parents rarely knew where I went. I never wore a helmet and was often out past sunset. On family trips, my siblings and I rode in the back of our station wagon, with no seatbelt of any kind. My parents didn't worry about me because no one ever told them that I was in any danger. Since that time, a string of events has led to some major changes in how children are raised. My grandchildren cannot even conceive of having the freedoms I had as a youth.

It is believed that these changes began in 1983, when the account of the abduction and murder of a young boy named Adam Walsh became a made-for-television movie. It was viewed by a record-setting audience. Photos of child abduction victims were soon emblazoned on the side of milk cartons. By 1985, every state required that children ride in car seats. In 1994, many states enacted laws requiring helmets for bicyclers, and we are now seeing helmets worn by skiers, skaters, and sledders. In 1996, the AMBER alert was initiated, so that whenever a kidnapping occurred, alerts could be broadcast through radio, TV, road signs, and cell phones.[2]

Worry, Anxiety, and Fear

At about the same time, studies showed that America's children were not keeping up academically with their counterparts in other countries. Would our children ever be able to compete on a global scale? Parents were at their wits' end. Within a few years, raising and educating their children had become a responsibility that seemed to require the utmost anxiety and oversight.

Parents started walking their children to school, through the front door, and, if allowed, into the classroom itself. Any dangerous activity, like bicycling, was strictly monitored and chaperoned. Fear continued to build. Kidnappings have always made great news stories, so the media covered them in detail. The term "helicopter parents" was coined in 1990 for parents who constantly hover over their children. More recently, we hear the term "snowplow parents" who clear obstacles for their children, even into college. Most young parents today are not even aware of the history of how parental anxiety has been magnified over the past thirty years. The resulting parenting style has been passed down to them from their parents and they know no other way. In the book *How to Raise an Adult,* we read a summary of where parents often find themselves today. "Too many of us do some combination of overdirecting, overprotecting, or over-involving ourselves in our kids' lives. We treat our kids like rare and precious botanical specimens and provide a deliberate, measured amount of care and feeding while running interference on all that might toughen and weather them. . . . And what of our own lives as parents? ("What life?" is a reasonable response.) We're frazzled. Worried. Empty."[3]

Remember, anxiety is an emotional fear of what might happen. The fear doesn't have to be rational. Parents tend to accompany their children everywhere now. Rarely do we see lone children anymore, apparently for fear of kidnappers. But this fear is grossly exaggerated. Though we hear of child abductions, the vast majority of them are parental kidnapping, such as occur in custody disputes. Since 2010, the FBI reports that the United States averages fewer than 350 kidnappings of youth (under the age of twenty-one) per year by strangers.[4] Doing the math, if there are 329 million people in the United States and 27.7% of them are under twenty-one years of age,[5] the odds of a true kidnapping are about 1 in 260,000. For comparison, the chances of your son being struck by lightning in his lifetime in 1 in 15,300—or about seventeen times the probability of being kidnapped.[6] Yet young parents will continue to walk their children to school because anxiety does not really care about odds.

From a recent *Time* article, we can see that parental anxiety, especially in mothers, is still an ongoing issue. "Anxiety is a silent epidemic among American mothers. It is debilitating, but normalized and even socially sanctioned. We've come to confuse fear with love, and the pursuit of zero risk with responsible parenting."[7]

A Child's Mentality

Throughout this book, I hope I have emphasized the importance of mental health and peace of mind. Fear is obviously detrimental to both and can have long-lasting effects, even after the initial fright has passed. Parents should take their children's mentality more into consideration when making decisions. For example, if there was a proposal to install a walk-through metal detector in the lobby of your neighborhood elementary school, would you support it?

The knee-jerk reaction may be to support *any* effort to ensure the protection of our young children. But let's look a little deeper into the question. There are about 89,000 elementary schools in the United States.[8] Only a very few of these schools have ever had shootings occur in them. (Neither locked doors nor security systems prevented the attacks anyway). So, one must ask, what is the probability that a metal scanner will make our children more secure? On the other hand, when the students learn that this metal detector is being installed to keep bad men from bringing guns into the school to shoot them, what is the probability that these children are going to feel threatened and less secure? Why would we ever suggest to elementary children that such violence in their school is even possible? Every time they walk past the metal detector, these elementary children will be reminded that bad men want to hurt them. What will happen to the peace of mind of these children? Is the small likelihood that a metal detector will help protect our children worth the anxiety it will most certainly bring into each child's life? A child's mentality is very important, and we should not strike fear in our children's minds in an effort to keep them safe from near-impossible parental fears.

Anxiety Does Not Foster Spirituality

To give it its due, anxiety and worry may help motivate you to pray. But when it comes time to pray about your anxieties, you might want to keep your descriptions short. Bringing your anxieties to the forefront of

Worry, Anxiety, and Fear

your mind can only cause you more stress, which is not what prayers were designed to do. Describing your anxieties to the Lord will generally only cause you further anxiety. First, your Heavenly Father is already aware of all the problems that are afflicting you (see Matthew 6:8). Second, by dwelling on your anxieties, you are going to walk away from your prayer more upset than when you began it. Prayer is supposed to calm your mind and your spirit. It is supposed to be a good experience that you anticipate for the peace it brings you.

The scriptures tell us that neither your Heavenly Father nor your Savior wants you to worry or be anxious. After all, worrying and anxiety conflict with the doctrine that "men are, that they might have joy" (2 Nephi 2:25). So we are told throughout the scriptures to "fear not."

> Therefore take no thought, saying, What shall we eat? or, What shall we drink? or, Wherewithal shall we be clothed? (For after all these things do the Gentiles seek:) for your heavenly Father knoweth that ye have need of all these things. But seek ye first the kingdom of God, and his righteousness; and all these things shall be added unto you. Take therefor no thought for the morrow: for the morrow shall take thought from the things of itself. Sufficient unto the day is the evil thereof. (Matthew 6:31–34)

> Therefore, *fear not*, little flock; do good; let earth and hell combine against you, for if ye are built upon my rock, they cannot prevail. (D&C 6:34; italics added)

> *Fear not*, little children, for you are mine, and I have overcome the world, and you are of them that my Father hath given me; And none of them that my Father hath given me shall be lost. (D&C 50:41–42; italics added)

If Ye Are Prepared . . .

We have all heard the expression that "if ye are prepared, ye shall not fear." Often this encouragement is used to promote food storage or increased spirituality. But the whole verse from where this excerpt is taken reads, "I tell you these things because of your prayers; wherefore, treasure up wisdom in your bosoms, lest the wickedness of men reveal these things unto you by their wickedness, in a manner which shall speak in your ears with a voice louder than that which shall shake the earth; but *if ye are prepared ye shall not fear*." (D&C 38:30; italics added)

111

The preparation that the Lord is recommending is that you gather wisdom and prepare yourself mentally. From the preceding verses of the quote above, we learn that the Lord is specifically warning the Church that it needs to know the hearts of their enemies. To make an important distinction, in this verse the Lord never offers to provide the names or plans of those enemies. God is not encouraging Church leaders to pray and try to receive such inspiration. The Church is being instructed to make the physical efforts needed to learn and prepare. The Lord gives the same encouragement in a later section.

> Teach ye diligently and my grace shall attend you, that you may be instructed more perfectly in theory, in principle, in doctrine, in the law of the gospel, in all things that pertain unto the kingdom of God, *that are expedient for you to understand*; Of things both in heaven and in the earth, and under the earth; things which have been, things which are, things which must shortly come to pass; things which are at home, things which are abroad; the wars and the perplexities of the nations, and the judgments which are on the land; and a knowledge also of countries and of kingdoms—That ye may be prepared in all things. (D&C 88:78–80)

The general principle is that when you learn, you come to know the things that are expedient for you to understand. You can even understand the perplexities of the nations, so news from foreign lands is not a surprise. You are prepared.

Being prepared with adequate food storage is still a good idea. Being spiritually prepared is also a good idea, though there is only so much you can do to be so. As a people, we are going to need more knowledge of the gospel and a better understanding of what God wants us to accomplish in this life. Throughout our history of crises, wars, and natural disasters, people have abandoned their faith in God in seeming retribution for the devastation they had to endure. People who do not know or understand why catastrophes occur are not prepared. I am not suggesting that you go purchase a book on how to better understand the book of Revelation. While interesting, John's revelation about 2,000 years ago is very complex with much symbolism. Better, we need to study and comprehend the premortal world, earth life, the gospel, the afterlife, and eternal life. When we can pull together that understanding, we will come to see what challenges must come to pass and how we can be prepared for them when they arrive.

Coronavirus

We will never be able to calculate the cost of the coronavirus crisis to the world in terms of mental health. The media advised us of every new statistic as viral infections increased around the world. Fear and anxiety ran rampant for months. Some of the most fearful people battled one another in store aisles for toilet paper. But other people, especially our medical providers, sacrificed their time and risked their own health to help others. It is during the most difficult times that we show our true character and mental/spiritual strength. Pandemics are not new to this earth, but they are new to our current generations. We have never seen anything like this biological threat, and fear is turning lives upside down. How do we not worry about a danger to our lives and those of our loved ones?

The purpose of our discussion to this point has been that mental health is necessary if your spiritual health is to thrive. To answer the question of how to stop feeling anxious in the middle of a pandemic, we are going to have to reverse this premise. In such crises, your mental self needs to turn to your spiritual side for support and encouragement. As an example of this pursuit, let's consider the most anxiety-inducing future event most Christians can think of—the Apocalypse.

Apocalypse Anxiety

Many good Christians are highly anxious about having to endure the final days of the Apocalypse. The name of The Church of Jesus Christ of *Latter-day* Saints reminds us of the possibility of witnessing the events described in the book of Revelation. However, even as He taught about the trials of the days preceding His Second Coming, the Savior gives us encouragement *not* to be anxious about it. In Luke 21:10–17, the Savior describes the wars, earthquakes, famine, and pestilence of the last days. He also foretells that His followers will be persecuted, jailed, betrayed, and hated. These verses (and the whole book of Revelation) have the potential of creating loads of anxiety among those reading them. Then the Savior reassures us, "But there shall not an hair of your head perish. In your patience possess ye your souls" (Luke 21:18–19).

In Luke 21: 20–26, Jesus continues His descriptions of the desolation that will come and that those alive will see signs in the sun, moon, and stars. Men's hearts will fail them from fear and from witnessing the signs of the times coming to pass. Even the powers of heaven will be shaken. But then, He assures us, "And then shall they see the Son of man coming in a cloud with power and great glory. And when these things begin to come to pass, then look up, and lift up your heads; for your redemption draweth nigh" (Luke 21: 27–28).

Finally, in the book of Revelation, John the Beloved documents his symbolic vision of the Apocalypse. Even heavily symbolized, it is quite apparent that none of the world wars or the coronavirus will match the final days before the Second Coming. In Revelation 8–11, we read of seven angels whose trumpet blasts bring hail, fire, falling stars, a darkening sun, smoke, death, and earthquakes. But then, after all of this is accomplished, we read what happens in the end: "And God shall wipe away all tears from their eyes; and there shall be no more death, neither sorrow, nor crying, neither shall there be any more pain: for the former things are passed away" (Revelation 21:4).

The mystery is solved! We know what is going to happen at the end. The end of the world as we know it is rather like reading a mystery novel that you spoiled by jumping ahead and reading the last pages. You know how everything turns out. The suspense is gone. But your spiritual self has to have a strong testimony of this end result. If your emotional mind starts to get nervous, your spirit should continually remind it that there is no reason for concern. If you have a testimony of the gospel, your spirit should have great confidence in the final outcome.

President Russell M. Nelson tells a story about when he was traveling in a small commuter airplane and an engine caught fire and exploded. The plane started to spiral down out of control. He mentioned how sorry he felt for one woman who became uncontrollably hysterical. President Nelson reported that he was calm, even though he knew he might die within a few minutes. He was ready to meet his Maker. President Nelson refers to Luke 21:26, which describes that in the latter days men's hearts will fail them for fear. But we do not need to have such fear if we recognize "with an eternal perspective that all will be well."[9]

I was once in a similar, though not as dangerous, situation as that of President Nelson. I was also traveling in a small commuter airplane when we entered a major storm cloud. The buffetings were intense, the plane rose and fell like a roller coaster, and lightning flashes filled the cockpit. One woman in the back of the plane became uncontrollably hysterical. I feared she might actually run to the plane door and try to open it to escape. I got up, sat down next to her, and held her hand until it was all over. I, like President Nelson, was calmer than I expected to be. I even remember feeling perturbed that this woman was making such a fuss. Afterward, I recognized that, perhaps like President Nelson, I had faith that I knew the ending of the story of Earth life. Had my plane crashed, I would have missed my family terribly, but it would have been only temporary. We would be reunited. In any story, it is the longterm ramifications of the plot that's important. I would have an eternity of time to catch up with my family. It is amazing what that realization does to your outlook on life and fear of death.

In Luke 21 and the book of Revelation, the attitude of the text is that "it's all good in the end, so why worry?" I know that having this attitude is harder than it sounds. Your emotional brain is naturally fearful of discomfort and death. Your rational brain may accept the fact that the world has turned upside down, but it will probably downplay the likelihood that it will affect you personally. All that is left to comfort your mind is your spiritual self, which must step up and insist to your mental self that all will be well in the end. Can your spiritual testimony influence your mood and your optimism for the future? It can. The voice of the Holy Ghost may only be one voice in your head, but it is the voice that you have practiced hearing your whole life. That spiritual side of you can help your brain deal with these difficult times. Do you have the faith to not be anxious in our new and dangerous world?

ENDNOTES

1. Korb, *The Upward Spiral*, 39–40.
2. Amber Alert Website, amberalert.ojp.gov/
3. Julie Lythcott-Haims, *How to Raise an Adult* (New York City: St. Martins Griffin, 2015), 7.
4. reuters.com/article/us-wisconsin-missinggirl-data/kidnapped-children-make-headlines-but-abduction-is-rare-in-u-s-idUSKCN1P52BJ
5. Census data, census.gov/popclock/
6. weather.gov/safety/lightning-odds
7. Sarah Menkedick, "Postpartum anxiety goes undiagnosed," *Time* magazine, March 30, 2020, 16.
8. National Center for Educational Statistics, statista.com/topics/1733/elementary-schools-in-the-us/
9. "Men's Hearts Shall Fail Them," video, *Inspirational Messages,* The Church of Jesus Christ of Latter-day Saints churchofjesuschrist.org/inspiration/latter-day-saints-channel/watch/series/mormon-messages/mens-hearts-shall-fail-them-1?lang=eng.

CHAPTER 12

Drugs and Medications

No discussion of the brain would be complete without discussing drugs and addiction. The dangers of recreational opiates, the legalization of marijuana, and the health effects of intoxication and nicotine regularly make headline news. Many people have either dealt with their own personal addictions or that of family members or friends. So, to more fully understand our brain, we need to be aware of the drugs used to alter it. Actually, your body comes with a special filter to try to keep your brain as isolated and pristine as possible. Known as the blood-brain barrier, the blood vessels in your head have a special coating to keep your brain tissue from being exposed to bacteria or other toxins that your blood might bring in with it. Your brain is fragile, and this barrier is designed to keep out infections, toxins, and other chemicals. As one brain researcher explains, "Instead we've evolved what's known as the blood-brain barrier—a physical barrier between the blood circulating in the rest of our bodies and our brain. Endothelial cells line the capillaries in the brain, preventing most compounds from moving between the blood and the cells of the brain. Molecules such as oxygen and hormones are small enough to pass through, but most bacteria, viruses and toxins are kept out."[1]

So, how do we get drugs into our brains that we want there? Drugs designed to affect your mind, be they medicinal or recreational, must accomplish two tasks. Once they enter your bloodstream, drugs must pass through the blood-brain barrier and gain access to your brain. Secondly, they must be able to mimic the normal neurochemicals that bind to the synapses in your brain. To your synapses, nicotine looks like acetylcholine, a normal chemical in your brain that regulates your brain activity. Alcohol looks like glutamate and aminobutyric acid, also very normal brain neurotransmitters. To the brain, cocaine and amphetamines appear similar to dopamine. One brain scientist explained how cocaine and other abused drugs work: "What makes cocaine *cocaine* is the fact that its accidental shape happens to fit lock-and-key into the microscopic machinery of the reward circuits. The same goes for all four major classes of drugs of abuse: alcohol, nicotine, psychostimulants (such as amphetamines), and opiates (such as morphine)."[2]

Lastly, drugs must be highly pleasurable. The brain has evolved processes that reward the body for good decisions that help continue its survival. Drugs, using vulnerabilities in this system, hijack those reactions and initiate their own pleasurable responses. The neurochemical pathway must lead to a pleasurable feeling so the presence of the new drug can be enjoyed by the consumer.

Each of us has a "rewards center" in our brains that is responsible for providing us with pleasurable sensations. When you are doing something noteworthy that helps your body (such as eating, having sex, or even just relaxing in your favorite chair), your pleasure center releases dopamine as a reward. Your brain wants to encourage you to repeat accomplishments that make you healthy, happy, and more likely to survive. Most drugs are designed to simulate that rewards center process. Normally, dopamine and related neurochemicals make you feel content and happy for a few seconds. Drugs mimic this effect, but they can continue to reward you for longer periods of time. To better understand addiction, let's consider a few of the major drugs used throughout history and start with the oldest drug of them all—alcohol.

Alcohol

There is evidence that fermented beverages existed as far back in time as ancient Egypt. Alcohol has been used around the world in multitudes of different beverages as a relaxant and party drink. Most people recognize their limits of consumption. But others simply cannot stop drinking and routinely become intoxicated. Organizations such as Alcoholics Anonymous have been created to help people overcome their addiction. The abuse of alcohol has destroyed countless lives, caused innumerable fatal car accidents, and broken up far too many families.

How does alcohol, specifically ethanol, interrupt our normal brain function? As one writer explained,

Drugs and Medications

Alcohol directly affects brain chemistry by altering levels of neurotransmitters—the chemical messengers that transmit the signals throughout the body that control thought processes, behavior and emotion. What this means for you is that your thought, speech and movements are slowed down, and the more you drink the more of these effects you'll feel. But here's the twist: alcohol also increases the release of dopamine in your brain's "reward center." Once a compulsive need to go back again and again for that release is established, addiction takes hold.[3]

Alcohol slows the speed of neural transmission. Your ability to process sights and sounds and then respond to them is significantly delayed. For those people who want to feel pleasure, being continually drunk may be an enjoyable pastime. If you have more worthwhile goals than being mentally impaired, then alcohol is a serious interruption in your life's work.

Nicotine

Nicotine also passes through the blood-brain barrier and interrupts the normal chemical processes that form our thoughts and emotions. Sadly, the most common way to ingest nicotine is by smoking tobacco, which allows the drug to pass into the bloodstream through the lungs. As we well know, smoking brings other toxins into your lungs as well. Those toxins damage cells and can cause some of them to become cancerous. Incredibly, smoking is still the leading cause of lung cancer. For some, the pleasures of nicotine outweigh the increased chance of an early, painful death. Obviously, nicotine is a very addictive drug.

Nicotine affects the neurotransmitter acetylcholine and its receptor. Because nicotine is shaped similarly to acetylcholine, it can fit in the same receptors and act just like acetylcholine. This change in balance causes the brain to "think" there is too much acetylcholine and react by reducing the number of receptors and releasing less acetylcholine into the synapse. The brain now needs nicotine to maintain normal functioning. In order to feel normal, the user has to keep his or her body supplied with nicotine. This is addiction. Nicotine also activates the reward circuits that are part of the limbic system, producing a pleasurable feeling, as well as causing a surge of the neurotransmitter dopamine in these circuits.[4]

Caffeine

Coffee and tea have been recognized as stimulants since 1650, when Thomas Willis, a pioneer of brain study, observed how coffee affected his friends. Coffee seemed to give Willis' associates more energy, "all sleepiness being driven away, doth produce unwonted waking."[5]

From the time we wake up, our brains naturally produce a neurochemical called adenosine. When adenosine binds to its receptors, neural activity slows down, and you start to feel tired. As adenosine continues to build up and binds to more receptors, it causes you to feel sleepy, with the goal of gradually preparing you for a good night's sleep. Caffeine hijacks this natural process by blocking adenosine from binding. It latches onto the receptors designed for adenosine, preventing the chemical from doing its job of slowing us down. As a result, we feel more alert and awake. Caffeine also triggers the release of epinephrine, dopamine, adrenaline, and noradrenaline, neurochemicals that cause you to feel content and energized.

Such stimulation acts as a reward to the tired mind, creating a physical dependence to wake you up in the morning and keep you energized through the day. Coffee shops depend on that need to stay in business. Given the overworked minds that we have developed in the past couple of decades, it is not surprising that caffeine consumption is higher than ever.

Marijuana

Due to its legalization in many states, the addictive effects of marijuana, or cannabis, have been hotly debated in the past decade. Marijuana can be smoked or eaten to achieve the effects of its active ingredient delta-9–tetrahydrocannabinol (THC). There is an entire feedback system in the brain called the endocannabinoid (EC) system. It was discovered during research on marijuana, so the names for the parts of the system all have the cannabis word root in them. At the axon terminals of the signal-*sending* neuron, there are cannabinoid receptors CB-1 and CB-2. Immediately after the signal-*receiving* neuron has received its signal, it produces endocannabinoid neurotransmitters which are sent across the synapse gap and bind to those CB-1 and CB-2 receptors. This induces the signal-sending neuron to take a break. It acts as a feedback system to prevent neurons from firing repeatedly and overloading the whole nervous system. After a few seconds of downtime, the endocannabinoids are released from their receptors, so the neurons can fire again.

Drugs and Medications

However, when someone has consumed marijuana, their CB-1 and CB-2 receptors are completely overwhelmed by THC. The receptors cannot reset and the regulatory endocannabinoid system is essentially shut down. Generally, as your neurons slow down, users become more relaxed. THC's action also activates the brain's reward system, releasing high levels of dopamine that produces relaxation and then euphoria.

Cannabis causes its own version of intoxication, impaired judgment, slow reaction time, and disrupted memory. Despite claims stating otherwise, marijuana is addictive. The official name for this addiction is Cannabis Use Disorder (CUD). Numerous claims have been made that cannabis has beneficial health effects. But the FDA has only approved cannabis products for treatment of chemotherapy-induced nausea and seizures. No other benefits have been proven. [6]

Cocaine and Opiates

Cocaine and other opiates produce the most intense sensations in the brain, providing alertness, self-confidence, and euphoria at higher doses. Not surprisingly, the opiates also cause the strongest addictions. About 130 people die every day from opiate drug overdose.[7] Massive government-sponsored ad campaigns have been launched to convince youth to stay away from drugs. In 1987, the most famous commercial of this campaign showed an intact egg with the caption, "This is your brain." Then a sizzling skillet was shown with the caption, "This is drugs." The egg was then broken and its contents poured into the skillet with the caption, "This is your brain on drugs." It was a well-chosen metaphor and a very thought-provoking message.

Cocaine works by blocking the transporters that normally escort dopamine, serotonin, and norepinephrine back into the axon terminals. By blocking this transport, dopamine and other neurochemicals spend more time binding to the synapses. By keeping these reward neurochemicals in the neuron's synapses, the person is more alert yet more blissful at the same time. Despite knowing its dangers, the number of people trying heroin and other opiates is increasing each year. Prescription opioids, such as hydrocodone (Vicodin°) and oxycodone (OxyContin°, Percocet°) are used medically to treat moderate to severe pain in patients requiring pain management. Obviously, such medications are very beneficial in helping these patients. However, since these drugs can also put users into a blissful euphoria, similar to the effects of heroin, they have found their way into recreational use.[8]

121

Medications

Generally, after a discussion about drugs, the conclusion is that drugs are evil. Indeed, abused drugs have caused much pain in the world. Even recognizing that fact, there are times in our lives when we need to alter the functioning of our minds. Opioids are very helpful in managing pain after a knee replacement or heart surgery. Medicinal drugs also use your brain's synapses to alter your brain chemistry, thus treating mental issues and bringing relief to many patients.

A number of people are afraid of medications. For example, many pregnant women, as they approach the birth of their babies, choose to not have any drugs at all to help them manage the pain, choosing to tough out the delivery. However, we should realize that all medications must go through a vigorous testing program for safety and effectiveness before the Food and Drug Administration (FDA) will approve their release. We shouldn't fear medications. Personally, I take a sleep aid every night. I realize the medication affects my brain chemistry and am very grateful for it. Medications and pharmaceuticals are safe and should be considered blessings of the time in which we live.

Antidepressants

As discussed earlier, a stigma may exist for some about taking antidepressants. But these medications are just like those used to keep your body balanced and functioning correctly. Some medications can be short-term, used only when the patient feels symptoms. Other times, medications must be used continuously. In either case, your doctor is trying to maintain the body's chemical balance. For example, I take medication to reduce the amount of cholesterol in my body. My condition cannot be permanently fixed, so I will be on this drug for the rest of my life. But since it will extend and improve my life, I am happy to pay that price.

Numerous books will tell you that you can fight depression without drugs. If your depression is not severe, this may be true. But pharmaceuticals have been developed to improve our lives—and your options in fighting depression are limited. Ignoring medications in a battle with depression is like rejecting a lifeline thrown to you in a rescue attempt. You can find hundreds of anecdotes on the internet on how depression medications are bad for you and what "Big Pharma doesn't want you to know." Please don't allow such reports to make you fear one of your

Drugs and Medications

best options for overcoming depression. Rather, have a heart-to-heart discussion with your physician and follow his advice. The medications prescribed to fight depression were chosen because they have been effective for millions of people. Your doctor went through years of medical school and residency to become an expert in healthcare. You can trust him.

Physically, clinical depression is caused by lower concentrations of key neurochemicals—specifically serotonin and norepinephrine. Nearly all the pharmaceutical treatments for depression are designed to maintain normal levels of these two neurotransmitters in your neurons and synapses. The most common treatment of depression is a class of drugs called Selective Serotonin Reuptake Inhibitors (SSRIs). As mentioned earlier in the primer on brain function, once a neurotransmitter has bonded to its receptor, it is then released, to be recovered by the transmitting neuron. The SSRI prevents this reuptake from occurring, thus keeping the serotonin active in the synapse. "Mixed reuptake inhibitors" prevent serotonin, norepinephrine, and dopamine from being sequestered.

A second class of depression treatment medications is designed to block norepinephrine from binding to its receptors. It is believed this blocking action prompts the cells into producing more norepinephrine. A third option for depression medication both blocks receptors *and* inhibits neurochemical uptake. Yet another set of medicines inhibits the enzyme that breaks down norepinephrine and serotonin in the cells. Besides all those medications that target depression, there are other prescriptions for treating mood swings or anxiety. As you can see, there are numerous possibilities for treating depression. Effectiveness of each treatment will depend on the patient, so it can take a physician several months to figure out the right regime of medications. The optimal prescription may also be a moving target for the doctor as your brain chemistry will change with time. Despite delays and occasional prescriptions that don't help, it is important for the patient to maintain their efforts and work toward a solution with their doctor.

Drugs and Spirituality

There is often a spiritual cost to using certain drugs. Whether you are drunk, a little high on pain medications, caffeinated, needing a smoke, or using a sleep aid, your mental capabilities—and certainly your spiritual side—can be impaired. Scripture reading and prayers will not be as spiritual. Fortunately, the effects of all drugs wear off with time, freeing your mind of its effects and allowing for spiritual prayer and meditation. However, if you are not feeling the Spirit in your prayers, you may need to consider the clarity of your mind. During and after a physical ailment, surgery, or a child's birth, is not the time to expect spiritual manifestations. During those times, it is easy to forget what real spiritual moments feel like and decide that God is simply not talking to you anymore. Please know that an essential part of the communication process of prayer, your brain, is simply not functioning well.

If you can reduce the drugs that cause mental distraction before prayer, then you should probably do so. If you can't reduce your level of medications, then be patient and seek out your moments of greatest clarity to offer your prayers and seek the Spirit.

ENDNOTES

1. Indre Viskontas, *Brain Myths Exploded: The Great Courses*, (Chantilly, Virginia: The Teaching Company, 2017), 21–22.
2. Eagleman, *Incognito*, 205.
3. David DiSalvo, "What Alcohol Really Does to Your Brain," *Forbes* magazine, Oct. 16, 2012.
4. National Institute of Health, National Institute on Drug Abuse; drugabuse.gov/publications/brain-power/grades-6–9/legal-doesn%27t-mean-harmless-module-2/background.
5. Zimmer, *Soul Made Flesh*, 107.
6. "FDA Role in Regulation of Cannabis Products," February 2019, fda.gov/media/128156/download.
7. drugabuse.gov/drugs-abuse/opioids/opioid-overdose-crisis
8. drugabuse.gov/publications/research-reports/heroin/scope-heroin-use-in-united-states

CHAPTER 13

Sensory Addictions

Drugs change how you think and, therefore, what you do. A drug's organic structures allows it to mimic the normal neurochemicals in your head and, however pleasurable it might be, throws off the chemical balances in your brain. But you don't necessarily need to put drugs in your body to effect changes in your brain chemistry. You can do it through your senses.

As we have discussed, a significant portion of your brain is dedicated to monitoring your senses. Visual processing takes up about one-third of your brain by itself. What you see, hear, smell, taste, and feel are experienced and recorded in your brain. If the stimulus is pleasurable enough, your brain will encourage you to repeat the experience. For example, if you are walking down the street and smell lilacs, you will unconsciously take a much deeper breath than normal to further enjoy the scent. If an activity is pleasurable enough, your brain can become obsessed with re-experiencing it again and again. As your brain can be addicted to a drug, your brain can also become addicted to stimuli. Your brain learns and yearns, even if you don't want it to. Thus, your conscious mind must be aware of the potential addictive dangers that exist and practice some self-discipline.

Adrenaline and Dopamine

Most sensually based addictions involve adrenaline and dopamine. For example, thrill seekers are often called "adrenaline junkies" because adrenaline gives them the rush that they are seeking with each skydive, cliff ascent, or hang-gliding adventure. After they survive the adventure, extreme sports enthusiasts are rewarded with the release of dopamine from their rewards center. The combination of the two neurotransmitters is a powerful stimulant. Whereas physicians used to think of addiction as dependency on a drug, they now define it as "repeatedly pursuing a rewarding experience despite serious repercussions" in recognition of sensory addictions.[1] But you don't have to be a BASE jumper or whitewater enthusiast to yearn for the rush of adrenaline and dopamine. There are many less physically demanding ways to accomplish it—and most of them revolve around computers.

Media has changed a great deal in the past eighty years. For centuries, media (or mass communication) was limited to books and newspapers. Reading the printed word was the only way to gather information from outside your community. The first telephone was patented in 1876, and a new way to acquire information became available. But listening to your sister on the phone is not that different than listening to her speaking in the same room. It did not change our way of thinking.

The television was invented in 1927. Reception and visual quality was pretty poor at first. But resolution and screen size soon increased significantly. To make TV programs more entertaining, shows started jumping more quickly from one exciting scene to another. The culmination of this fast-paced entertainment can still be found in music videos, which holds one shot for only a few seconds before changing camera angles or the scene all together. This rapid scene change, the fast beat of pop music accompanying it, and sexualized content increases your adrenaline levels. You are certainly not bored. The flashing lights, music, and provocative dancing are exciting and stimulating. This adrenaline/dopamine binge can go on for hours, with your brain in hyperdrive the whole time. It's exhausting for your mind.

Television and Other Screens

When you read cautions about the dangers of too much screen time (television, video games, social media, and internet surfing) you probably think those cautions are directed only at children. After all, children have young minds whose development can be affected by the frantic pace of most cartoons, action movies, and sports events. Way back in 1999, the American Academy of Pediatrics (AAP) quoted studies that "the average American child or adolescent spends >21 hours per week viewing television. This figure does not include time spent watching movies, listening to music or watching music videos, playing video or computer games,

Sensory Addictions

or surfing the internet for recreational purposes." Somewhat alarmed at this statistic, the AAP posted their recommendation that children under the age of two should not have any screen time at all.[2] The AAP was roundly criticized for their policy, but later studies supported its conclusions. In 2011, the AAP suggested that children from two to five years old be limited to less than one hour of screen time a day.[3] Although the AAP recognizes that electronic screens are great distractions for toddlers, their official stance is that their use should be limited.

The debate has continued for many years, as has the increased use of electronic media. Statistics indicate that the AAP recommendations have been pretty much ignored. As quoted above, in 1999, children and adolescents spent about three hours per day with electronic media. By 2015, one census study reported, "All told, 8– to 12–year-olds spend an average of about four and a half hours a day with screen media, while teens spend just over six and a half hours a day with screens."[4]

So, for two decades the public has been taught that screen time should be limited for children. The warnings are still being given. In his book *Glow Kids*, author Nicholas Kardaras explains the dangers, especially for young people who play video games for hours, called "gamers": "Our brains are simply not designed for the visual hyperstimulation with which recently developed digital technology bombards us. In my work teaching neuropsychology, it is well understood that brain development is a fragile process that can be easily disrupted by both understimulation and overstimulation—such as the overstimulation that the brain of a gamer experiences."[5]

There are dangers to your brain that come with watching too much television. Those dangers increase as you add hours of screen time to surf the internet or be active on social media. But let's start with the worst of all screen addictions—the video game.

Video Games

Video games made their debut in 1958. In those early days, you could choose from such games as Pong or Pac-Man, which were entertaining and fast-paced for their time. But they were nothing like the games we have today. Today you can drive virtual race cars or fight for your life in virtual battles against Nazis, zombies, or other monsters. The action is unrelenting, requiring a total focus on the game. When you achieve a high score, you are praised and congratulated for your improving expertise.

Dozens of books have been written about the dangers of video games. Generally, we think of the worst video games as the violent, battlefield games that have become so popular. But the goal of any video game is to keep you jazzed and your mind on overdrive. For example, games like Minecraft, Candy Crush, and Angry Birds are simple and somewhat nonsensical. But they are also hugely popular. Though they are not especially violent or bloody, they are not soothing, relaxed games that allow your mind to detach and think pleasant thoughts either. The games require constant attention, focus, and quick response. Even the music that accompanies the game is fast-paced, high energy, and stress-inducing.

Parents of young children normally see these games as harmless. There have been reports that video games improve hand-eye coordination, contribute to healthy social interaction, and may even be educational. As Kardaras explains, "Over time, it became clear to me: the video game phenomenon was about kids seeking *something* and parents, albeit misguidedly, thinking that they were keeping their kids *safe* indoors."[6]

An interesting twist to your brain's pleasure center has been discovered. As you decide to pursue any given course of action, your brain will approximate and anticipate how much pleasure that action will provide you. If your expectation is met, then you are proportionately happy and receive the normal dopamine burst. But, if your expectations are unexpectedly exceeded, you get a disproportionate cascade of dopamine. With this reward, your brain strongly encourages you to continue whatever you were doing to repeat that dopamine avalanche. "That was GREAT!" your brain will think. "Let's do it again!"

Video game producers have learned how to use this disproportionate brain response in producing their video games. Changes were made, and today you will see many games that provide seemingly random and unexpected rewards during play. In a fantasy game, you may find a magical sword; in a battlefield game, you may chance upon a cache of ammunition. Your brain is delighted by this good fortune and encourages you to continue to play.

Video games put your brain on high alert status for long periods of time. One might argue that video games are not reality—there is no real danger. But most of your brain doesn't understand that. Adrenaline, dopamine, and stress hormones are being produced as if the action were real. How could your brain not be affected by such input? Youth play their games again and again, trying to develop their skills and tasking their brain to perform for longer and longer time periods. Their brain's rewards center is continually activated, and the brain molds itself to play the game better. When you finally stop the action, your brain will be grateful to have a chance to recover for a few minutes. But then it will want the action to continue. Normal life is incredibly boring compared to fighting zombies. The game offers excitement and the brain soon misses that stimulation.

For your brain, it is a bit like being on a roller coaster. There is danger, action, and the visuals change quickly. The difference is that no one would think about riding a roller coaster for an hour. The first few minutes would be fun, but the next fifty minutes would be physically exhausting. A video game holds your brain at the same level of activity as a roller coaster, but you are sitting on a comfortable chair or couch. Physically, you wouldn't beat your body up on a roller coaster for an hour. But many people are willing to beat up their brains for much longer time periods.

The damage of video games to a healthy mentality is really not under serious debate anymore. In 2009, the same American Academy of Pediatrics (AAP) published their report on the effects of media violence on our children. Their conclusion was that

> Exposure to violence in media, including television, movies, music and video games represents a significant risk to the health of children and adolescents. . . . The weight of scientific evidence has been convincing to pediatricians, with more than 98% of pediatricians in one study expressing the personal belief that media violence affects children's aggression. Yet the entertainment industry, the American public, politicians, and parents all have been reluctant to accept these findings and to take action. The debate should be over.[6]

Psychology professor Dr. Craig Anderson of the Iowa State University has conducted a number of studies on the effect of media violence on youth. He has found that habitual playing of violent video games leads to significantly increased aggressive behavior in school, whether the youth live in Japan or the United States.[7] From a psychological standpoint, this is not unexpected. The brain lays down certain patterns of behavior, whether the play is on the playground or in virtual reality. It then follows those patterns, also whether on the playground or in virtual reality.

Gambling

Why do we gamble? What characteristics of the brain make gambling fun and exciting? Most of the outcomes of gambling are based on chance, so why should we care? Whether we are playing poker, betting on a horse, or buying a lottery ticket, there is a natural human excitement in taking a chance and winning the prize. Gambling has been around for thousands of years. The writings of the Greek poet Sophocles contained the first mention of dice around 500 BC. The first playing cards appeared in China in the ninth century.[8] Really, you can gamble on anything—which horse will run the fastest, how dice will land, who is the better boxer, or who will get the best hand in a card game. Texas Hold'em poker tournaments are now regularly broadcast on sports networks and pay out millions of dollars to the winners. Gambling is a multi-billion dollar industry, with its capital city in Las Vegas. But gambling is available anywhere. You can gamble online or buy a lotto ticket at your nearest convenience store.

In the 1980s, the American Psychiatric Association listed gambling addiction as an impulse-control disorder. In 2013, they reclassified gambling addiction as real addiction, reflecting a better understanding of the biology underlying this addiction. Upon placing a bet, the gambler anticipates a favorable outcome. The competition and excitement of the moment stimulates the release of adrenaline. When the gambler wins, our favorite neurochemical dopamine is released into the brain and the gambler experiences a natural high. Whatever losses the gambler might have had earlier in the evening are forgotten. He is a winner! The brain wants to feel that exhilaration again and again. Just as substance addicts require increasing amounts of a drug to feel its effects, compulsive gamblers must pursue ever riskier ventures to get their next high. This addiction empties bank accounts and ruins families. Gamblers Anonymous was founded to help people find their way out of this destructive addiction.

Pornography

Pornography is also a sensual addiction. As noted, the pleasure centers of our brains provide special neurochemicals to reward us for behaviors that increase our odds of survival. Since procreation is so vital to the survival of a species, it is rewarded with several potent chemicals, including adrenaline, noradrenaline, dopamine, and oxytocin. Pornography masquerades as procreation. Because of the strong sensations caused by the act of reproduction, pornography soon becomes an addiction. Pornography, like gambling, has become very easy to access, as close as cable TV or a laptop.

Viewing pornography is generally seen as a problem only for males, but that diagnosis is outdated and incorrect. Google Analytics data from 2019 show that the audience for one of the world's most popular porn sites is 29 percent female. Other studies have confirmed that about 30 percent of women watch porn.[9] In either case, there are groups and counselors available to help reshape minds to be able to shake the addiction of viewing pornography. In the end, breaking the addiction requires strong self-discipline. But know that, with time and effort, the brain's inherent neuroplasticity will allow it to break out of the thought patterns that create the desire for pornography.

Social Media and the Fear of Missing Out

Mankind is a social animal, and we like to be liked. At the same time, we are a competitive species and we like being admired by others for our abilities and success. This desire for acclaim leads us to buy bigger houses than we need and fancier cars than we can afford. Many of us spend hours at the gym, have plastic surgery, and spend a lot of money on make-up and hairstylists—all to feel good about ourselves.

When friends compliment us on our looks and accomplishments, we get a dopamine burst. Before the development of digital photographs, our family reunions, vacations, and awards could only be captured on film-based photographs and video. Only friends who saw the photographs firsthand could appreciate our experiences. Since cell phones and social media were invented, you can post photos of your vacations, family, or even your latest meal for everyone to see. Friends, family, and other followers can "like" your posts and rave about them in their responses. Social media allows a flood of praise and compliments with each photo. Bursts of dopamine flood your brain. I don't mean to sound cynical. In reality, social media is fun and a good way to stay current with loved ones. Yet, as with any activity that can become a sensual addiction, you have to be aware if you are developing a dependency. Do you spend more time in the virtual world than you do in the real world? Do you think about your social media even when you aren't on your phone or tablet?

Time spent on social media can easily increase without you noticing. Facebook, Instagram, LinkedIn, and other social media sites constantly encourage you to expand your network of 'friends' and spend more virtual time with them. One might think that a lot of social activity, even if it is only online, will make one happy. But for many people the opposite is true.

> Facebook, with its 1.23 billion active users, has not led to happiness; instead it has led to a phenomenon known as "Facebook depression," whereby the more "friends" one has on Facebook, the higher the likelihood of depression. There is also, as mentioned, the double whammy that the more time spent on social media and the more texting a person does, the higher the likelihood of not *just* depression but tech addiction as well.[10]

Anyone who is a user of Facebook is probably not surprised by this finding. This phenomenon is also known as "social comparison," or the "class reunion effect." This may seem fairly innocuous. In essence, Instagram could be considered an online photo album. But each of us likes to feel successful—and success is all relative. For you to feel successful, others have to be comparative failures. So, social sites can become a never-ending competition as players judge who had the most fun vacations, who has the cutest children, and who has the best life. Such comparisons play to our insecurities, reduce our satisfaction with life, and add to our anxiety that we have wasted our time on earth. No wonder Facebook adds to depression.

If this is a good description of your feelings while using social media, maybe you should consider cutting back on your use. You need to guard your mental health.

ENDNOTES

1. scientificamerican.com/article/how-the-brain-gets-addicted-to-gambling/
2. Pediatrics, August 1999, 104 (2) 341–343; pediatrics.aappublications.org/content/104/2/341
3. "Media and Young Minds," *Pediatrics*, November 2016, 138 (5) e2016259, pediatrics.aappublications.org/content/138/5/e20162591
4. commonsensemedia.org/sites/default/files/uploads/research/census_researchreport.pdf
5. Nicholas Kardaras, *Glow Kids* (New York City: St. Martin's Griffin, 2016), 18.
6. "Media Violence," *Pediatrics*, November 2009, 124 (5) 1495–1503, pediatrics.aappublications.org/content/124/5/1495.
7. Kardaras, *Glow Kids,* 148.
8. "The History of Gambling," gambling.net/history.
9. Fightthenewdrug.org/survey-finds-one-in-three-women-watch-porn-at-least-once-a-week/
10. Kardaras, *Glow Kids,* 94.

CHAPTER 14

The Art of Meditation and Introspection

We are well into our discussions about the workings of your brain and spirit. What are you going to do with that information? Any new understandings you have gained will be of no worth if you don't incorporate them into your life. Unless you are willing to carry this book around with you, to incorporate new ideas into your life requires you to install them in your brain. To do that requires uninterrupted thought and contemplation. To be able to assess your mental health, you have to mentally review your brain and thought processes. You have to let your conscious mind communicate with the rest of your brain so it can voice its concerns and worries. To do that, you have to take some time to let your mind relax from its nonstop busyness. This process may sound familiar. It is called meditation.

Meditation was introduced into the mainstream of American culture during the turbulent 1960s and proceeded to make a terrible name for itself. Meditation was linked with a number of activities bent on self-realization and self-discovery. This was a fine goal—until seekers started to include the use of marijuana and psychedelic drugs in that same search to find themselves. Meditation became associated with mantras, hookahs, and hash pipes. Many people still picture meditation as something you have to do sitting on the floor in the distinctly uncomfortable lotus position. To fully appreciate the potential of meditation, we need to get past all the baggage that the word brings with it.

The Savior's Wilderness Meditations

A person goes "into the wilderness" to get away from the noise in the cities and to think and pray. The Savior went into the wilderness for two

133

apparent reasons. The first reason was to contemplate His ministry, make decisions, and plan. Shortly after His baptism, the Savior was led by the Spirit into the wilderness. Matthew 4:1 and Luke 4:2 make it sound as though Jesus went there only to be tempted by Satan, but Joseph Smith makes it clear the temptations occurred only after a time of fasting and prayer. Jesus was ready to initiate His ministry, and I imagine He had to make plans, so the subject of His fast is pretty obvious. Where should He initiate His ministry? How do you teach a stubborn Jewish people that you are the Son of God?

The second time the Savior went into the wilderness to make plans is found in Luke 6:12. In verse 13 we learn that He probably went there to choose His apostles. "And it came to pass in those days, that he went out into a mountain to pray, and continued all night in prayer to God. And when it was day, he called unto him his disciples: and of them he chose twelve, whom also he named apostles" (Luke 6:12–13).

The second reason Jesus went into the wilderness was apparently to take a break from the crowds, gather His thoughts, and commune with the Spirit. Luke, perhaps because he was a physician, reports Jesus's visits into the wilderness more often than the other Gospel writers. He also explains the possible reasons Jesus needed to get away. In Luke 4:37, Luke mentions Jesus's fame. We don't discuss it much, but one can only imagine what it was like during the Savior's ministry. Pressing crowds, many people hoping to be healed, were probably a daily occurrence. Just five verses later, Luke reports that the Savior tried to go into the wilderness, but was prevented by the people. "And the fame of him went out into every place of the country round about. . . . And when it was day, he departed and went into a desert place: and the people sought him, and came unto him, and stayed him, that he should not depart from them" (Luke 4:37, 42).

In the fifth chapter of his Gospel, Luke again describes Jesus's fame. In the next verse he mentions again how the Savior dealt with that fame. "But so much the more went there a fame abroad of him: and great multitudes came together to hear, and to be healed by him of their infirmities. And he withdrew himself into the wilderness, and prayed" (Luke 5:15–16).

The Savior went into the wilderness to pray, meditate, and commune with the Spirit. He found a quiet place, gathered His thoughts, planned, and prepared to continue His exhausting ministry. We should all seek to follow that example.

Meditation

Hundreds of books have been written about meditation. Many take meditation very seriously, with the goal of attaining a higher consciousness and spiritual enlightenment. For our purposes, meditation may be considered simply a way to spend some quality time with your brain. The goal of this entire book has been to communicate the dependence of your spiritual health on your mental health. If you never schedule time to check in on your mental self, you will never know the status of your mental health. The best one-word description for that activity is "meditation." But really, you *don't* have to sit cross-legged on the floor to meditate. From the book *Just Sit*, authors Sukey and Elizabeth Novogratz explain,

> Meditation isn't a way to stop your thoughts or empty your mind. Unless you're dead, the mind doesn't empty and thoughts don't stop. Meditation is a way to slow down and observe your mind, not kill it.
>
> Meditation is a way of training the mind to slow down, to be responsive, not reactive, to bring you into your life and out of the constant chatter that's going on in your head. It is a workout for the mind, which means it takes work, practice, and discipline. And, like working out, results do not come overnight. . . . Just like a new exercise program, you have to start, jump in, just do it.[1]

As you meditate, realize that you will still have multiple voices chiming in from different parts of your brain. You need to use that fact to your advantage. For example, as you calmly consider a problem, first examine it with the emotional side of your brain. Emotionally, what do you feel you should do with this problem? Your emotions are important to you and should be given voice during meditation. Then, examine the problem with your thinking, rational mind. What is the logical way to approach this problem? Finally, examine the problem with the spiritual side of your brain. Is there a moral dilemma to this problem? Are any of these choices unacceptable to your conscience? Eventually, you can learn to quiet the voices that don't represent your priorities. You can learn to recognize decisions that your emotional core and your logical mind will eventually regret. Meditation allows you time and quiet to consider your decisions. It doesn't matter if you meditate on the hard floor or in your favorite overstuffed chair. The purpose of meditation, no matter how you do it, is to give yourself some quality time to think about your mental state. Set a goal to clear your mind of the minutia that is causing you stress. Don't meditate when you are exhausted. Many good ideas for improving your life will be summarily dismissed by a brain that is too tired to commit to the effort required. Finally, it goes without saying that this is a good time to confirm that you are doing everything possible for your mental health. Are you eating healthy foods? Are you aware of your use of electronic media?

Meditation seems to be a learned skill. First, you find a comfortable spot, close your eyes, and relax. This relaxation may take longer than you expect. My own mind takes the opportunity to remind me of pending chores, communications, and responsibilities. To silence those thoughts, I have learned to keep a small notebook and pen at my side to write down those reminders my mind is obsessing over. Only when they are written down can I dismiss those to-do items from the stage of my mind and address my more serious concerns.

As aspects of your life come to mind, I encourage you to examine each one and decide if it is causing you grief, happiness, or stress. As mentioned in earlier chapters, your mind changes with each day of your life. So your feelings about your job, spouse, family, ambitions, and goals will change. You allow each issue its own time on the stage of your mind. What are your present worries, insecurities, and difficulties? Are you dealing with them the best way you know how? Do you have the power to change these negative aspects of your life? This last question is of vital importance. Many people, including myself, are "fixers"—we want to fix whatever is broken in our home, family, country, and world. Though we can use the little bit of influence we have to shape it, our world often moves on without heeding us. Our children become adults and make their own decisions. If I were to suggest a mantra during meditation, it would be the Serenity Prayer: "God grant me the serenity to accept the things I cannot change; the courage to change the things I can; and the wisdom to know the difference."[2]

I have to remind myself that, while I will do my part to help my family, my community and earth, there are few problems that I can actually fix. Hopefully, accepting that fact each day will take some of the stress out of life.

Meditation is meant to be a time to gather thoughts and examine your life. Are you at peace with where you are in life and what you are doing? This is never a simple question, and the answer keeps changing. There are simply too many factors and priorities in a normal life. Life can

The Art of Meditation and Introspection

be exhausting, and you must balance your desires and expectations with those of your family, your workplace, your home, and your God. So you should try to sort out that life each day to keep it on track. Don't be afraid to go "into the wilderness" yourself sometimes.

Meditation Is Not Prayer

Please note that meditation is not the same thing as prayer. In prayer, you are actually conversing with your Heavenly Father and there is pressure to pay attention to Him. The expectation of giving attention to a conversation tends to distract from effective meditation. Faithful Church members often cannot resist the urge to tend to their spiritual side and forget that their mental state deserves its own focused attention. Seeking the Spirit is a noteworthy goal—but not during your mental assessment time. Stay focused on sorting out your thoughts. Prayer can wait its turn, and it can be something you do right after meditation.

I have offered a lot of very poor prayers in my life. If a serious problem has just arisen, my thoughts are scattered and my emotions are a mess. This is not a good starting point for prayer. If you were going to appear before the president of our country to make a request, you would undoubtedly prepare for that meeting. You would review your list of needs and make sure your petition represented them. Should a prayer be any different? The most effective prayers are those for which you have organized your thoughts and are ready to present them to the Lord. You can end the review of your challenges and plans to meet them with the question, "Is this what I should do?" I have often felt that the Lord appreciates efforts to prepare to talk with Him. Meditation followed by prayer can be a powerful combination.

Introspection

A simple definition of meditation is to engage in thought or contemplation. The definition of introspection is the "observation or examination of one's own mental and emotional state" (Dictionary.com). Throughout these pages, I have endeavored to create a separation between the conscious mind of the reader (the part of you that is reading these words) and the rest of your brain (subconscious, memories, emotions, and so on). Introspection is the ability of your conscious mind to turn around and view itself and the rest of your brain.

Several years ago, I was talking to my adult daughter and congratulating her that she had been able to learn introspection as a child. She had gone on to graduate with a degree in psychology, and I knew her to be adept at understanding her own thoughts and motivations.

"I hate it," she responded. "I am constantly evaluating the reasons behind what I say and do." Here I thought I was being complimentary.

"However," I retorted, "introspection is better than being totally clueless about *why* you say what you say and do what you do." From that conversation, I realized that there is a balance you should seek in your introspection. You don't want to be constantly engaged in brooding and soul-searching. You don't want to be hypersensitive to your every thought and word. But you do want to take time to reflect on your life and how you are living it.

I am not a psychologist, but I know from my own life that one event can affect your outlook far beyond what you might expect. Fairly recently, I lost my job on the same day I made a presentation to my team that I thought would be favorably accepted. This unexpected reversal caused me more mental distress than I realized at first. For several weeks after, my self-confidence was shot and I found myself much more emotional than normal. My own introspection allowed me to see that I needed to be patient and let time heal this mental and emotional injury. Fortunately, I had a loving family and God who were there to help me deal with this bump in the road. It was a frustrating time. But, as I came to realize, it was also a temporary setback, as most all such disappointments are.

Knowing Is Half the Battle

From 1983 to 1986, an animated series called *G.I. Joe: A Real American Hero* was broadcast on network television. This cartoon followed the exploits of a special missions force called G.I. Joe in combating the efforts of Cobra, a terrorist organization bent on world domination. Each show concluded with a short public service announcement that taught lessons about child safety. In each video, children would be doing something dangerous and a G.I. Joe hero would appear and explain the risk. The children would then exclaim, "Now we know!" and the G.I. Joe hero added, "And knowing is half the battle."

Meditation and introspection share this same moral with G.I. Joe. When you ponder your mental and emotional states, you will have insights into what is going on inside your mind. Those insights are

The Art of Meditation and Introspection

invaluable as they identify anxieties, fears, and concerns which may be affecting your attitude and mood more than you realize. Knowing really is half the battle. Once identified, your problems can be addressed under the light of that new understanding.

ENDNOTES

1. Sukey and Elizabeth Novogratz, *Just Sit* (New York City: HarperCollins, 2017), 3.
2. Serenity Prayer, attributed to Dr. Reinhold Niebuhr (1892–1971), Union Theological Seminary.

CHAPTER 15

Being Mindful of Your Mindedness

So far, we have discussed ways to understand and maintain mental health, recognizing that the right mentality is necessary to maintain good spiritual health. Maintenance of mental health in today's world is not easy. From a turbulent global environment to your cell phone disrupting your few calm moments, maintaining an optimistic and stable mentality is more challenging than ever before. But, it is now time to discuss practices that enable us to raise our mental/spiritual health to a higher level. This goal will include the avoidance of damaging environments. It will certainly mean kicking damaging thoughts and patterns out of your head and trying to find more enlightening ones to take their place.

You have many options as to what kind of mindedness you want to pursue. You can be small-minded by having rigid opinions, or you can be narrow-minded by not tolerating other people's views. You can be absent-minded when you forget things. You can be strong-minded, single-minded, or open-minded. You can be almost any "-minded" you want to be. Paul presents another way of considering the two extremes of mindedness in his letter to the Romans: "For to be carnally minded is death; but to be spiritually-minded is life and peace" (Romans 8:6).

Thus, we will set being carnally minded as one extreme and being spiritually minded as the other extreme of this continuum. I expect only a few people normally reside at either extreme, so most people fall somewhere in between them. You can also rank your mental thought patterns as low or high. The highest thought patterns belong to the Lord. "For my thoughts are not your thoughts, neither are your ways my ways, saith the Lord. For as the heavens are higher than the earth, so are my ways higher than your ways, and my thoughts than your thoughts" (Isaiah 55:8–9).

The 'altitude' of your thoughts depends on what you think about and your environment. What do you and your friends talk about? What do you read or watch on television? In what kind of environments do you spend your time? Raising your thoughts to higher levels is the first step in raising your spirituality, because the two are so bound together.

Carnally Minded

Another way to describe being carnally minded is to be low-minded, which is a person who is "vulgar or sordid in mind or character."[1] Synonyms for low-minded also include base, dishonorable, and vile. One of the best examples of an exceptionally carnally minded people was the Nephites during their final war with the Lamanites. As Moroni describes their awful condition, "And they have become strong in their perversion; and they are alike brutal, sparing none, neither old nor young; and they delight in everything save that which is good" (Moroni 9:19).

What delights your mind is a very good indicator of your mentality. Generally, we delight in the good things of life and when other people are happy. When a people get to a point where they only delight in the evil and brutal things of the world, then they are indeed at the lowest point of being carnally minded.

The Lord gives us many scriptural warnings about our mentality, though they are rarely recognized as such. First, let's consider a few mentalities that the Lord wishes you to avoid.

Avoid Profanity

While waiting for a plane at the gate of an airport, I overheard a very upset twenty-something young woman crying as she talked to a friend on her cell phone. Apparently, this woman had just been kicked off her plane during boarding because she had gotten angry over something and used excessive profanity with the stewardesses. She was very upset at her ill fortune in not being able to make her trip. She did not think she was at fault because, as she told her friend, "You know me. I can't control using profanity when I get mad!" With all due respect, I beg to differ with this young woman's self-assessment.

We live in a day and age when profanity has worked its way into normal conversations. But in decades past, profanity was used only to express extreme emotion, usually anger. The theory was that the emotion was so intense that the speaker simply could not prevent using an expletive. Often, there was an apology to others standing nearby, such as, "Excuse my swearing," or "Pardon my French." Profanity has become so common that we don't hear such apologies anymore. Profanity takes any conversation and makes it cruder. One would never think of using profanity in a conversation about the gospel. The two don't mix. Similarly, using profanity drags down any attempt to lift your mental thought patterns to a higher level. Thus we should seek to not use it.

I love science fiction. With profanity becoming so common, I have often wondered about the reaction of an alien species that was approaching Earth and monitoring our airways and communications. Would they wonder why the human race is so preoccupied with excrement and reproduction that we mention them so very often? When these aliens arrive on our planet, would they ask us about our fascination? What could we possibly say in response? We'd have to answer that we take words that are too crude to use in polite company and voice them, often loudly, to add emotion to our words. Somehow, we might explain, emotion excuses crudeness. I can only expect the aliens might change their conclusion that earth is a civilized planet, pack up, and leave.

The question one must consider is, "Do I want my brain to express itself with profanity?" Because like every other activity you practice regularly, profanity will carve its way into your thought patterns. To help pay for college, I worked on a construction crew over a couple of summers. Discussions were all laced with an excess of profanity. During those summers of exposure, it was alarming to me how easily profanity came to my own mind, ready to be verbalized. But the profane young lady at the airport was wrong—you can control using profanity. You simply have to run every word through your conscious mind before letting it leave your mouth. It is a practice called "choosing your words carefully." Granted, this requires some self-discipline and speaking a little more slowly. However, the subconscious mind will eventually work profanity out of its patterns as well, and this oversight by the conscious mind will become less necessary.

Light-Mindedness and Idle Thoughts

Light-mindedness is a mental attitude that "makes light" of any serious aspects of life. It assigns no priority to spiritual pursuits. Sabbath observance, reverence, prayer, magnifying a calling, and gospel study are considered too slow and serious. Light-minded people usually mock any part of life that is not entertaining or fun.

When my youngest son was at the age when a young man thinks that witty responses all involve sarcasm, I pulled him aside and pointed out to him that sarcasm is really easy. You could respond, "Well, duh!" to comments all day long and be successfully sarcastic. Young men of the same age may even think your comments are funny. But sarcasm is rarely witty or amusing. Light-mindedness is an attitude much like sarcasm, mockery, and ridicule. Nothing is deemed to be important, so nothing needs to be taken seriously. Light-mindedness often turns into ridicule of the efforts of others to be reverent, respectful, and righteous. It can further evolve into sacrilege, blasphemy, and a deliberate irreverence for the things of God.

Modern scripture defines light-mindedness as trivializing the sacred or making light of holy things. Latter-day Saints were admonished early in the history of the Church to "trifle not with sacred things" (D&C 6:12; 8:10). There are multiple scriptures in which the Lord commands us to control our thoughts, for the very logical reason that our words and actions spring from them (Mosiah 4:30). As discussed in chapter 4, the Lord expects mental discipline from each of us.

> Therefore, cease from all your light speeches, from all laughter, from all your lustful desires, from all your pride and light-mindedness, and from all your wicked doings. (D&C 88:121)

> And your minds in times past have been darkened because of unbelief, and because you have treated lightly the things you have received. (D&C 84:54)

Idle thoughts are much like light-mindedness. All of us have thoughts that flit through our minds when we are resting in the sun and daydreaming. The problem occurs when we never break ourselves out of the daydreaming state. The definition of the word *idle* is "without purpose or effect, pointless, frivolous, trivial, petty, and superficial."[2] The Lord doesn't want you to be idle, to think idle thoughts, or to speak idle words.

> Remember the great and last promise which I have made unto you; *cast away your idle thoughts* and your excess of laughter far from you. (D&C 88:69; italics added)

> For as he thinketh in his heart, so is he." (Proverbs 23:7)

For our words will condemn us, yea, all our works will condemn us; we shall not be found spotless; and *our thoughts will also condemn us.*" (Alma 12:14; italics added)

Idle thoughts and light-mindedness create deep patterns, or better said, ruts in your brain. It is not surprising that the scriptures condemn idle thoughts and light-mindedness so often. They are the starting point for regrettable words and actions.

Idle Words

Being light-minded at least has the advantage that your idle thoughts remain in your brain where they can't hurt anyone else. More serious problems occur when those thoughts are verbalized to hurt and offend other people. By that offense, idle words reap a greater penalty than idle thoughts. The dictionary defines idle words as "empty rhetoric or insincere or exaggerated talk."[3] Idle words also include profanity, vulgar stories, blasphemy, gossip, and vain babblings (see 1 Timothy 6:20). Idle words, like idle gossip, pull other people down. Whether we are criticizing others or complaining about life in general, idle words usually reflect a negative attitude. Such speech not only depresses those around you, but it also forces you into an even deeper depression. By verbalizing negative thoughts, you validate them as well, further convincing yourself that life is miserable. If you want to be happier in your own mind, you should seek to voice only your best thoughts. The Lord has given us fair warning about idle words.

But I say unto you, That *every idle word* that men shall speak, they shall give account thereof in the day of judgment. For by thy words thou shalt be justified, and by thy words thou shalt be condemned. (Matthew 12:36–37; italics added)

Not that which goeth into the mouth defileth a man; but that which cometh out of the mouth, this defileth a man. (Matthew 15:11)

The prophet Joseph Smith recognized that even his own discussions with other Church leaders of his time were not at the level the Lord may expect. "How vain and trifling have been our spirits, our conferences, our councils, our meetings, our private as well as public conversations—too low, too mean, too vulgar, too condescending for the dignified characters of the called and chosen of God."[4]

145

Obviously, even Joseph wanted his thoughts and words to be on a more spiritual level, as should we all.

Murmuring

Murmuring is defined as a half-suppressed or muttered complaint. Such complaints are usually muttered because the people complaining don't want to draw attention to themselves; they just want to complain. Often the murmurers never take their complaints to an authority for resolution. They continue to bask in their anger and frustration, letting it grow and continuing to feel they have been wronged and mistreated.

When Oliver Cowdery lost the ability to translate, he was not happy and apparently started grumbling about his mistreatment. The Lord responded with an entire section in the Doctrine and Covenants to address his complaints: "Do not murmur, my son, for it *is wisdom in me* that I have dealt with you after this manner" (D&C 9:6; italics added).

When Emma Smith was not allowed to see the plates upon which was written the Book of Mormon, she was unhappy as well. The Lord also addressed a whole section of the Doctrine and Covenants to her, giving her encouragement and counsel: "Murmur not because of the things which thou hast not seen, for they are withheld from thee and from the world, which *is wisdom in me* in a time to come" (D&C 25:4; italics added).

It is interesting that the wording of the counsel to Oliver and Emma are very similar. First, the Lord encourages them to not murmur, explaining that it "is wisdom in me" that Oliver not translate and Emma not see the plates. Basically, the Lord was telling Oliver and Emma that they could not see the bigger picture at the time. There were reasons behind the Lord's actions and they had to trust Him.

Murmuring words are often designed to convince other people of your plight, have them feel sorry for you, and be angry as well with the authority that is afflicting you. The murmurer is looking to convert people to his cause. But, instead of approaching those in authority to resolve their complaints, murmurers hold their anger close to them and keep it secret. This creates a mentality much like that of "secret combinations." Murmurers complain and thus undermine the authority of those they believe are causing their complaints, be they government or Church officials. Murmuring represents a mentality that is not conducive with spirituality or happiness.

Loud Laughter

We have yet another word that requires better definition—laughter. In the verse cited earlier (D&C 88:121) the Lord discourages laughter along with light speeches, lustful desires, pride, light-mindedness, and wicked doings. This inclusion rather flies in the face of teachings that man is that he might have joy (see 2 Nephi 2:25). In many talks at the biannual general conferences of the Church of Jesus Christ, our leaders make jokes and funny observations meant to provoke laughter. So it doesn't make sense to think that the Lord disapproves of laughter. To be specific, the Lord dislikes "loud" or "excess" laughter (see D&C 88:69). Loud laughter is boastful, often forced laughter, as you might hear in a rowdy bar. As Hugh Nibley explained it, "Loud laughter is the hollow laugh, the bray, the meaningless laugh of the soundtrack or the audience responding to prompting cards, or routinely laughing at every remark made, no matter how banal."[5]

Joyful laughter, however, should be a major part of our mentality. The Old Testament tells us that there is "a time to weep, and a time to laugh" (Ecclesiastes 3:4). The Savior said, "Blessed are ye that weep now: for ye shall laugh" (Luke 6:21). From the *Encyclopedia of Mormonism*, we read: "In practice, Latter-day Saints distinguish light-mindedness from light-heartedness; the latter is a triumph of the zestful, joyful spirit of the gospel over life's trials. Such cheerfulness and good humor do not preclude, but rather can complement, spirituality. The Church counsels against a light-minded attitude toward sacred matters but encourages joyfulness in worship and wholesome pleasure in recreation."[6]

Joyful laughter is an expression of the happiness and appreciation of being alive. Such laughter often seems to come from one's very spirit, in recognition that the earth is a great place to live out our mortal existence. Loud laughter is the exact opposite, representing a false bravado designed to impress others doing the same thing. By carefully choosing your words and laughter, you make it clear the mentality you have chosen for yourself.

Seek the Virtuous and Lovely

If we were to identify one statement to summarize the goal of staying spiritually minded, it would be found in the articles of faith. In his book on the subject, James Talmage wrote that Joseph Smith "set forth as an epitome of the tenets of the Church the thirteen avowals known as the

'Articles of Faith of The Church of Jesus Christ of Latter-day Saints.'"[7] Talmage goes on to recognize that these thirteen articles are an "authoritative exposition" and a "guide in faith and conduct" for the entire Church today. In the last sentence of the last article of faith, the prophet Joseph summarized what should be our goal as a person seeking for spiritual enlightenment: "If there is anything virtuous, lovely, or of good report or praiseworthy, we seek after those things."

Joseph purposefully borrowed some of Paul's wording from his letter to the Philippians (see Philippians 4:8). Both Paul and Joseph encourage us to seek after those things that are "virtuous, lovely, or of good report or praiseworthy" because they raise our mentality and spirituality to a higher level. The world around us is full of selfishness, ambitions, pride, and other weaknesses of the human condition. If we let these things pull us down, they can overwhelm us, sinking our mind and spirit to the level of the world. On the other hand, if we seek to immerse our minds in the virtuous and lovely things of life, our minds rise and with it, our spirits.

Mindfulness is defined as "a mental state achieved by focusing one's awareness on the present moment, while calmly acknowledging and accepting one's feelings, thoughts, and bodily sensations."[7] *Mindfulness* is a rather trendy word right now and is used in a number of therapy, self-help, and meditation books. Despite its overuse, the concept should be given its due attention. Mindfulness starts with self-awareness, which we discussed in the chapter on introspection. But active mindfulness should also include efforts to find means to improve the health of your mind.

ENDNOTES

1. ln/definition/low-minded
2. lexico.com/en/definition/idle
3. vocabulary.com/dictionary/idle%20words
4. *Teachings of the Prophet Joseph Smith*, 137.
5. Hugh Nibley, excerpted from "Eloquent Witness: Nibley on Himself, Others, and the Temple," ldsliving.com/search/author_search?q=Hugh+Nibley%2C+excerpted+from+%22Eloquent+Witness%3A+Nibley+on+Himself%2C+Others%2C+and+the+Temple%22
6. *Encyclopedia of Mormonism*, eom.byu.edu/index.php/Light-Minded-ness
7. James Talmage, *Articles of Faith, 50th edition* (Salt Lake City: The Church of Jesus Christ of Latter-day Saints), 6.

CHAPTER 16

Scriptural Advice for Treating Depression

Hundreds of books have been written on how to manage and treat depression. There is little I can add to that advice. But as I read those instructions, I was surprised to find them resonating with multiple scriptures that give the exact same advice. It appears that the steps to achieving higher spirituality are similar to those of treating mental depression. The following advice is taken from a few of the books written on treating depression, with corresponding scriptures that encourage the same behaviors.

You may have read the scriptural advice below many times. You probably think that following these recommendations will allow everyone to get along and be happy. Often that is true, of course. However, for the purposes of treating depression, we should view managing anger, forgiving, and fellowshipping as highly *selfish* acts. You forgive people because you need to defuse and discard the memory that poses a constant danger to your mental well-being and happiness. You accept fellowship because you are a social animal and need the interaction. To care for your brain, don't pass up any opportunities, even if it means quelling your ego and other emotions, to help clean your mind of unneeded, distracting emotions.

Maintain Your Physical Health

The fact that a physically healthy lifestyle improves mental health hardly needs repeating. If your body is sending signals to the brain that it is tired, hungry, nauseous from too much deep-fried food, craving nicotine, or stiff from lack of exercise, your mind will be distracted and more anxious. Thus we are given the advice from doctors and the Lord to eat

149

Manage Your Anger

Controlled anger can be a powerful motivator. Rarely is anger recommended when dealing with other people. However, anger at a nagging problem can give you emotional energy to make a hard decision you have been putting off. Uncontrolled anger and outrage are strongly negative emotions and ruin lives. They are also very unhealthy for you. Stress hormone levels peak and adrenaline spikes. Your heart races and blood pressure soars. Rational thinking is ignored and you can say things to loved ones that you will profoundly regret later.

If you refer to the Savior's Sermon on the Mount, you will find numerous verses recommending that you love your fellow man and not become angry with him.

> Blessed are the meek, blessed are the peacemakers. (Matthew 5:5, 9)

> Whosoever is angry with his brother without a cause shall be in danger of the judgment. (Matthew 5:22)

> Agree with thine adversary quickly. (Matthew 5:25)

> Whosoever shall smite thee on thy right cheek, turn to him the other also. (Matthew 5:39)

In conclusion, try to handle your anger. Many lives and relationships have been ruined from the consequences of one outburst of uncontrolled anger. Wrath is specifically excluded from the gospel plan, and it can only add to depression. Anger management classes encourage the rational, thinking part of the brain to shut down the emotional side of the brain as soon as possible before it does something rash or even hurtful. As mentioned, anger is very hard on your body. Blood pressure spikes and stress hormones increase drastically. Risk of heart attack and strokes are three to five times greater when a person gets angry.[1]

Cope with Grief

Obviously, this directive is easier said than done. Especially in the face of the loss of a loved one, we should grieve. But we need to look forward to the time we can stop grieving. Personal tragedy has triggered numerous cases of long-term depression and suicides, further compounding the devastating effects of the original misfortune. It is up to your conscious mind to fight back the waves of grief that the emotional part of your mind is feeling. It is one of the most difficult feats of mental strength imaginable. Basically, your mind must decide to allow itself to move on. You must decide to have hope in the future—something the scriptures highly recommend.

> For we are saved by hope: but hope that is seen is not hope: for what a man seeth, why doth he yet hope for? But if we hope for that we see not, then do we with patience wait for it. (Romans 8:24–25)

> If ye continue in the faith grounded and settled, and be not moved away from the hope of the Gospel. (Colossians 1:23)

Learn to Forgive

Recommendations for overcoming depression all have a central theme. They all suggest that you endeavor to rid yourself of stressful, negative emotions such as outrage, anguish, or being offended at someone. Such feelings can consume you and never allow your brain to relax and be content. The worst aspect of holding a grudge is that it recreates negative emotions and stress hormones *every* time you think about why you were angry. It is like having a mental booby-trap in your brain. Every time you let your thoughts meander onto the memory of your grievance, you spring the trap and negative emotions explode in your head. We have several scriptures that encourage us to forgive, well, everyone.

> And forgive us our debts, as we forgive our debtors (Matt 6:12)

> I, the Lord, will forgive whom I will forgive, but of you it is required to forgive all men. (D&C 64:10)

> Then came Peter to him, and said, Lord, how oft shall my brother sin against me, and I forgive him? till seven times? Jesus saith unto him, I say not unto thee, Until seven times: but, Until seventy times seven. (Matthew 18:21–22)

You may have heard the expression "forgive and forget," but it is nonsense. Your brain remembers highly emotional and negative events much better and for longer times than any other memories. So, you will probably *never* completely forget an insult, but you can reduce your emotional response to the memory. Offense, stress, and anger are close friends. A desire for mental calm should give your conscious brain sufficient reason to push the emotional brain to overcome its anger. It may take a little time, because all the voices in your brain must agree to make the effort. But it needs to be done. For your own sake, forgive others and enjoy the calm.

Control Stress

Most stress is self-imposed. After all, you don't live in a day and age where one mistake can mean that your family will not survive the winter. Author Richard Carlson explained this concept in the title of his book, *Don't Sweat the Small Stuff. . . and It's all Small Stuff,* which was a best-seller about twenty years ago. His descriptions of life are even more relevant today:

> In short, we live our lives as if they were one great big emergency! We often rush around looking busy, trying to solve problems, but in reality, we are often compounding them. Because everything seems like such a big deal, we end up spending our lives dealing with one drama after another.
>
> Happily, there is another way to relate to life—a softer, more graceful path that makes life seem easier and the people in it more compatible. This "other way" of living involves replacing old habits of "reaction" with new habits of perspective.[2]

We have similar instruction from the scriptures, as discussed earlier in the chapter about worry and anxiety. In conversations I have had with friends about the stress in their lives, their conclusion is often that nothing that can be done about it. They must hold down their job, they must care for their family, and so on. All of these reasons are true, but most of these friends have more flexibility in their schedules and more resources at their disposal than they use. Stress is a state of mind, and you must use your mind to stop living a life as if everything is an emergency.

Keep a Journal

A journal is a private diary where you can put your feelings into words. Writing in a journal is therapeutic, as it helps you to sort through your emotions with your conscious mind. Purposefully writing down your thoughts and emotions helps you to recognize your own moods and emotional battles. Writing them down makes them more real and addressable. Writing a journal can be considered a form of meditation that also provides an outlet for your emotions and thoughts. It also provides an opportunity to count your blessings and realize you have overcome past challenges.[3]

Writing your personal history or keeping a journal has been recommended for many years in the Church. It allows you to keep a record of your challenges and blessings. Thus, don't write in a journal and then store it away in the attic. You should read your own journals on occasion as well. The stories will remind you that you have faced other difficulties in the past and survived them just fine. Reading your journal can help you assess in what direction your life has been heading since you wrote those words. As the word implies, a journal can chronicle your life's journey and give you hope for the future.

Avoid Comparisons

From 1984 to 1995, a television show called *Lifestyles of the Rich and Famous* was aired on network television. The show filmed visits to the elaborate mansions of very wealthy people, showing their sumptuous lifestyles, richly decorated homes, and huge swimming pools. I never really understood the point of this program. The tone of these guided tours seemed to be, "See what I have!" "Too bad you can't afford this!" and maybe, "Thou shalt covet." As millionaire Ted Turner explained, "Life is a game. Money is how we keep score." Apparently, how lavishly you spend all that money is how we announce the winners.

In contrast to that attitude, we might consider the line from *Desiderata*, a poem by Max Ehrmann: "If you compare yourself with others, you may become vain or bitter, for always there will be greater and lesser persons that yourself. Enjoy your achievements as well as your plans."

So, whether you win or lose in a competitive comparison, comparing yourself to others is a losing proposition. As we discussed in an earlier chapter, Facebook is a hugely popular way to compare yourself to others. Your friends get to take you on their own personal *Lifestyles of the Rich and Famous* with photos of their lives. In all fairness, your friends are almost certainly not trying to contribute to your Facebook depression with their photos and posts. But, be it a high school reunion or social media posts, we all want our friends to think that we have succeeded in life. If Facebook and other social media are causing you more depression than joy, perhaps it is time to remove yourself from the cycle.

Get Outside

Nature is almost always a mind-elevating experience. You can see and appreciate scenery that is astonishingly beautiful. You smell the fresh forest and appreciate silence that is only broken by bird calls and flowing rivers. It allows you to appreciate the planet Earth. In our life's journey, we don't look up enough. We are so concerned with taking each step carefully that we focus on our feet and the path before us. We don't want to stumble in our career or other responsibilities. But life can be pretty boring if you are looking at the ground all the time. We need to look up, take in the world's scenery, appreciate the night sky, and remember who put it all there for our enjoyment.

When God made His assessment of the earth in Genesis, He determined it was "very good" (Genesis 1:31). Considering He has probably seen more than a few worlds, this is high praise. It's a beautiful world, even as seen from your back yard.

Accept Fellowship

Depression may cause you to want to curl up in your home and not answer the door or the phone. But the medical community and the scriptures advise against this approach to life. "Years of research show that a strong social network is an important component of overall health. People who feel connected to others tend to be healthier physically. They have a stronger immune system and less risk of illness and death. Social ties also improve your mental health, giving you a sense of purpose or meaning."[4]

We need other people in our lives. Thus The Church of Jesus Christ of Latter-day Saints is divided into wards, such that we can regularly interact with our neighbors. One of the main reasons for Sunday worship is so that we can fellowship one with another.

In the New Testament, we have a series of letters that Paul wrote to wards all across the Church to give them direction and encouragement. At the end of several of those letters, he encouraged the members of the ward to greet each other with a "holy kiss" (Romans 16:16, 1 Corinthians 16:20, 2 Corinthians 13:12, and 1 Thessalonians 5:26). In his translation of the Bible, Joseph Smith changed the word *kiss* to *salutation* in all four books, perhaps to accommodate a more modern-day form of greeting. Peter encouraged Church members to greet one another with a kiss of "charity" (1 Peter 5:14). In all five books, it is apparent that the early

Scriptural Advice for Treating Depression

Church leaders encouraged ward members to fellowship one another with warm salutations.

Being of One Mind

If you are spiritually minded, it appears that your community should also be of one mind. As one might expect, the city of Zion was of one mind. "And the Lord called his people Zion, because they were of one heart and *one mind*, and dwelt in righteousness; and there was no poor among them" (Moses 7:18; italics added).

Even as the Savior approached the last night of His mortal life, He had to reteach the principle that his disciples had to be of one mind and not worry about their greatness in the kingdom. During the Last Supper Passover meal, the Lord's Apostles were arguing about "which of them should be accounted the greatest." This same subject had been debated before. In Mark 10:35–44, the Apostles had the same argument. The Lord had taught them, "But so shall it not be among you: but whosoever will be great among you, shall be your minister: And whosoever of you will be the chiefest, shall be servant of all" (Mark 10:43, 44).

So, again, during His last meeting with the Apostles, the Lord had to teach them that their concern for their future greatness was not the right attitude. The Savior had even washed the Apostles' feet as an object lesson that the greatest among them should serve His followers. Despite the lesson, Jesus was still very concerned that His Apostles would not work together. In His prayer in the Garden of Gethsemane, the Savior prayed for His Apostles to be of one mind: "And now I am no more in the world, but these are in the world, and I come to thee. Holy Father, keep through thine own name those whom thou hast given me, that they may be one, as we are" (John 17:11).

A bit later in the prayer, the Savior prayed for the other members of the Church. In *three* verses in a row (John 17:21–23), He asked the Father that His followers "may be one." Again, obviously it was important to Him that the Church be of one mind. The Lord spent a lot of time on this request in what could be considered the most important prayer in the history of the earth.

Fortunately, the Apostles did learn to appreciate the need for Church members to be of one mind. Both Peter and Paul encouraged congregations of the early church to be singular in their purpose to do good.

Finally, be ye all of *one mind*, having compassion one of another, love as brethren, be pitiful, be courteous. (1 Peter 3:8; italics added)

Finally, brethren, farewell. Be perfect, be of good comfort, be of *one mind*, live in peace; and the God of love and peace shall be with you. (2 Corinthians 13:11; italics added)

Being of one mind would have been an especially difficult task for the early church. Congregations were made up of converted Jews, Gentiles, Samaritans, Romans, and other cultures, some of whom had been idol worshippers before their conversions. Getting such diverse peoples to be congenial with one another was a constant problem for the early church.

If you think about it, being of one mind is necessary for a functioning congregation to exist. To provide for the welfare of all, everyone has to be of the mindset to contribute and do their part. Thus, being of one mind is not only an effect of a community of spiritually minded Christians, but it is also a requirement for Church service and welfare to continue to function. This book has been about caring for the health of your mind. Being of one mind with those good and faithful people around you will only help in that effort.

ENDNOTES

1. Ryan Jaslow, "Angry outburst may trigger heart attack or stroke within two hours," *CBS News*, March 4, 2014, cbsnews.com/news/angry-out-burst-may-trigger-heart-attack-or-stroke-within-two-hours.
2. Richard Carlson, *Don't Sweat the Small Stuff . . . and It's all Small Stuff* (New York City: Hachette Books, 1997), 1–2.
3. Spencer W. Kimball, "The Foundations of Righteousness" October 1977 general conference, churchofjesuschrist.org/study/general-confer-ence/1977/10/the-foundations-of-righteousness?lang=eng.
4. Keith Kramlinger, ed. *Mayo Clinic on Depression* (Philadelphia, PA: Mason Crest Publishers, 2001), 124.

CHAPTER 17

A Healthy Brain Is Key to Eternal Life

To summarize the reasons for life in five words or less, it seems we are on earth to "learn wisdom and choose righteousness."[1] We discuss choosing righteousness every week at Church services. We are taught, as we have discussed in an earlier chapter, to follow our conscience and choose to do those things we feel are just, fair, and honorable. When the scriptures ask us to choose righteousness, we are being encouraged to make the mental and spiritual choice to follow God.

> Wherefore, men are free according to the flesh; and all things are given them which are expedient unto man. And they are free to *choose* liberty and eternal life, through the great Mediator of all men, or to choose captivity and death. (2 Nephi 2:27; italics added)

> And if it seem evil unto you to serve the LORD, *choose* you this day whom ye will serve; . . . but as for me and my house, we will serve the LORD. (Joshua 24: 15; italics added)

> Behold, here is wisdom, and let every man *choose* for himself until I come. Even so. Amen. (D&C 37:4; italics added)

Interestingly, we don't talk as much about learning wisdom in church. We are encouraged to get a good education, such that we may gather knowledge. But learning wisdom, a mostly mental pursuit, is often portrayed as an afterthought to spiritually choosing righteousness. In reality, it is just as important. As an analogy to explain this concept, if you think about it, robots would make great Church members. Once programmed with the commandments, the need to attend church, and how to calculate tithing, robots could be active Church members. The robot could be prepared for choices in life with a number of if /then statements, which

157

are common in computer programming: if someone offers you a cigarette, then deny it.

Choosing righteousness is often not easy, but at least the options are limited. Unlike our robot, *you* have your conscience which will remind you what is right and good and what is wrong and evil. Hopefully, you were born of goodly parents and were taught somewhat in all the learning of your father. You have found and studied the commandments of God in your scriptures. In Church services, you are reminded each week to choose righteousness. From all of this repetitive instruction, you should be able to easily recognize righteousness and unrighteousness when you see them.

Learning wisdom is more difficult, because the choices are infinite. The wisest choice for one young man may be completely different than the best choice for his twin brother. For these reasons, we could never call a robot to carry out the responsibilities of be a bishop, stake president, or other Church leader. For such callings, one needs to have wisdom that cannot be summarized by an if/then statement. One must be able to apply learnings of the gospel to a large variety of circumstances and challenges that arise in member's lives. Part of gathering wisdom is simply a result of living life. As you age, you can't help but realize that some of your decisions turned out well and others were disasters. So, one can learn wisdom from life, which may explain why we associate wisdom with old age. But you can seek wisdom in other ways than by simply getting old and waiting for it. This fact has been recognized for centuries. An old Zen proverb, a verse from the book of Proverbs, and wisdom from Confucius are given credit for the following observations.

> It takes a wise man to learn from his mistakes, but an even wiser man to learn from others.

> Wisdom is the principal thing; therefore get wisdom: and with all thy getting get understanding. (Proverbs 4:7)

> By three methods we may learn wisdom: First, by reflection, which is noblest; second, by imitation, which is easiest; and third by experience, which is the bitterest.

Hopefully, after we leave our formal schooling, we can gradually convert that knowledge into wisdom. Before we leave the topic of the care and feeding of our minds, let's discuss the gathering of wisdom—and how in many ways it is more difficult than choosing righteousness.

The Need for Wisdom in the Afterlife

Throughout my life, I have known many righteous, dedicated members of the Church. They attended Church services every week, magnified their callings, and studied the gospel. By that measure, their lives have been a success. But some of these same faithful Church members have made some very poor decisions in their lives. We don't attribute these choices to unrighteousness. For example, giving your retirement savings to a con artist is not unrighteous. Neither is choosing to quit your job and blindly moving to a city ranked by a magazine as the best place to live in America. Making politically incorrect statements at work and losing your job because of it is not a sin. Choosing to eat sugary, high-fat foods and forgo exercise is not unrighteous. It might go against the spirit of the Word of Wisdom, but you won't be asked about it in an interview with a Church leader. You can make hundreds of very unwise decisions that would not be considered unrighteous.

For these righteous, though somewhat foolish Church members, I would not hesitate to throw open the gates of heaven. They have earned entry though their righteous choices. However, I would hesitate to give these same good Saints the priesthood power to create worlds. Knowing how to use authority and power requires understanding and wisdom. In considering the need for wisdom before gaining power, I often think of the Disney animation *The Sorcerer's Apprentice*. In this short film, Mickey Mouse plays a young apprentice to a powerful sorcerer. To shortcut having to do his chores, the apprentice borrows his master's magic wizard hat. The castle doesn't have running water, so Mickey orders his broom to haul buckets of water into the house for him. The broom gets started and Mickey drifts off into sleep. When he awakes from his nap, the broom has brought in so much water that the house is flooded. In the midst of the churning waters, Mickey grabs a large book of magic and furiously flips through its pages to find how to reverse his spell. Too late, Mickey! You needed to understand power *before* using it. The sorcerer finally arrives and uses his magic to clean up the mess. The moral of this story is that power should only be given to those who have the wisdom to know how to use it appropriately.

Some members of the Church believe that in the afterlife we will be able to absorb knowledge like a sponge, with much less effort than it takes here on earth. That would be great, I suppose. However, I don't believe it. The concept goes against several scriptures about the importance of learning, and my general belief that there is no free lunch. Study requires effort, which increases our appreciation of the knowledge we gain. As further study allows us to link our understandings of the universe and human behavior, our knowledge becomes wisdom. The process is too important to allow short cuts.

Learning wisdom is not the same thing as choosing righteousness. Learning wisdom requires effort outside of attending Church services. Wisdom can come as a result of making bad decisions that ruin you financially, wreck your health, or antagonize family and friends. That is the hard way to learn wisdom. The easier way to get wisdom is to gain knowledge 1) by reading good books in broad areas of interest, 2) by talking to wise people and procuring their advice, and 3) by meditating about your decisions before making up your mind. Let's consider each recommendation one at a time.

The Value of Knowledge

In Moses 5:6, an angel of the Lord appears unto Adam and asks, "Why dost thou offer sacrifices unto the Lord?" I have always wondered if the angel's question was a quiz question to which Adam should have known the answer or a rhetorical question that was a lead-in into a Gospel Doctrine lesson. In any case, Adam replies, "I know not, save the Lord commanded me." This verse is almost always quoted as a great example of faith, which it is, of course. Adam was following a commandment, but he didn't know what his obedience meant. However, blind obedience is *not* the ideal situation in which to live the gospel. When we worship, it is better to know what we are doing and why we are doing it. Faith is a wonderful starting point for learning, but faith should be replaced by knowledge as soon as possible.

In the very next verse, the angel immediately clears up Adam's lack of knowledge and tells Adam, "This thing is a similitude of the sacrifice of the Only Begotten of the Father, which is full of grace and truth" (Moses 5:7). The angel goes on with the lesson, probably explaining a lot more than is recorded in the book of Moses. In the end, Adam had a very spiritual day, and it all began with learning the reasons behind a commandment.

We are to be a learning people (see D&C 90:15). There is much to learn about the gospel, earth life, sociability, and how we should act. We attend church to listen to other's ideas and teachings so that we can learn new perspectives on the gospel. We want to learn as much as we

A Healthy Brain Is Key to Eternal Life

can, since knowledge improves both our testimony and our minds. "And now, behold, is your knowledge perfect? Yea, your knowledge is perfect in that thing, and your faith is dormant; and this because you know, for ye know that the word hath swelled your souls, and ye also know that it hath sprouted up, that your understanding doth begin to be enlightened, and *your mind doth begin to expand*" (Alma 32:34; italics added).

It's pretty easy to understand that if you don't work a muscle, it will weaken. Likewise, if it is not used, your brain will atrophy as well. To convert faith to knowledge, we need to learn words of wisdom, which come out of the best books. "And as all have not faith, seek ye diligently and teach one another words of wisdom; yea, seek ye out of the best books words of wisdom; seek learning, even by study and also by faith" (D&C 88:118).

There is a certain confidence that comes with gathered knowledge. You realize that your understandings are based on a good foundation of facts and revelations. One Sunday, I was teaching a church class of adults when a newly married fellow questioned one of my teachings and briefly explained his outdated understanding of the subject. The rest of the class confirmed my original explanation to him, which obviously dazed and upset him a bit. When I asked him from where he had gotten his interpretation of this doctrine, he answered, "From my Primary teacher!" He had believed his misunderstanding of an important doctrine for years and was shaken when he learned that it was wrong.

While the Book of Mormon is a great book that members of the Latter-day Saint Church should read, it should not be the *only* book that we read. Gather wisdom. Read books. Your brain will feel more accomplished, you will add to your faith, and your ability to understand our purpose in life will be strengthened.

Procure Good Advice

I have always found it interesting that most every leadership position in the Church—the prophet, stake presidents, bishops, Relief Society presidents, and so o—all have counselors. In a church that believes in answers to prayer and inspiration of our leadership, why would a Church leader need counselors? The answer, of course, is that sometimes the Lord wants His children to make their own decisions, even when they involve leading His Church. When that happens, it is good to have sage advice from people you trust.

So, if the prophet has counselors to help him make decisions, it is probably a good idea to have counselors of your own to help make your decisions. Everyone has had different life experiences, so there are assuredly blind spots in your education and experience. Many questions arise in life that you never even knew existed until you have to answer them. Often, the best wisdom is to find a wise person who has answered a similar question in the past. We can find wisdom in good books, but we can also learn wisdom from good people. You will probably make the easy and less important decisions in your life all by yourself. But to understand the weightier matters of life, such as career choices, family leadership, and even politics, you may want to consult with others.

If you have just been called to a leadership position, you have an opportunity to learn much. But be prepared to expand your horizons a bit. You will have the opportunity to talk to people what are not likeminded with you. To gather wisdom, you must be willing to consider opposing viewpoints, which is less comfortable than talking to people who confirm your own beliefs. In today's world, such open-mindedness has become increasingly rare. There was a time when political debates were held between different political parties to inform the public of the strengths and weaknesses of each side of an issue. Today, such debates have become shouting matches, no longer designed to present alternatives. It is hard to find balanced reporting of current events from our media. In the pursuit of wisdom and understanding, do you listen only to those people who already confirm your viewpoint? If you are a political conservative, are you willing to listen to the conclusions of a progressive liberal? Are you willing to step out of your comfort zone to come to a better understanding of how other people think?

Gathering wisdom sounds great, but it is not for the faint of heart. It does not mean going to a mountain retreat in China to study with Shaolin monks. It does mean reading or listening to books that expand your horizons. It means coming to understand both how wise and righteous people can still vigorously disagree with one another. It means helping those same people to be of one mind in following God and supporting His Church. Isaac Asimov, one of my favorite authors of all time, once stated, "The saddest aspect of life right now is that science gathers knowledge faster than society gathers wisdom."[2] I have to wonder if that same statement can be made about me as well. I gather a lot of knowledge, but I find that I only rarely process that information into a better understanding of myself, my universe, and how other people think.

A Healthy Brain Is Key to Eternal Life

Meditate on Your Decisions

We have already discussed meditation as a recommended way to appraise your own thoughts and clear your mind. Meditating on your own decisions and examining them for weaknesses and unnecessary risk is a step toward gathering wisdom. When someone makes a really bad decision, we often say that this person didn't think that through very well. Don't let that be said about your decisions.

You can learn wisdom from every decision you make, if you are willing to audit how that decision turned out. If you blame bad luck for a bad decision, you will learn less from your assessment. If you do not recognize good luck (or God's blessings) in a successful decision, you will also learn less in your review. When were you wise? When were you foolish?

Some people are proud of the fact that they simply follow their gut instinct. As we have discussed, allowing the emotional mind to have a say in a decision is always a good idea. You have to 'feel right' about your decisions. But a good decision will still be good after you have thought about it for a while. Your rational mind should be allowed to seek for flaws in a decision and edit the decision accordingly. To do that takes uninterrupted time for thought and appraisal, also known as meditation.

ENDNOTE

1. Frazer, *Angry with God*, 27.
2. brainyquote.com/quotes/isaac_asimov_107635

EPILOGUE

Though it will hopefully be influenced by your spirit, your brain will make your final, eternity-determining decisions. As an important part of your worship, you need to be aware of your mind's importance and give it the due attention it deserves. You're depending on your mind to be the central hub for your emotions, thoughts, loves, personality, and your spirit. For such an important part of your being, your brain doesn't require that much time to maintain it. But maintain it you must, especially in this day and age when sustaining a positive outlook is so challenging.

Much of the mental and spiritual depression we are seeing today can be traced back to the constant busyness and stress that enters our lives through our laptops and cell phones. Mind you, your electronic devices themselves are not to blame. They are just following their programming. The problem is what you do with all the incoming email, texts, video games, and social media posts that come through your electronic devices. If responding to your correspondence, pointing, clicking, scrolling, and reposting takes most of your day, maybe such days are negatively affecting you more than you imagine. Think about it. Even better, meditate about it.

If you are feeling depressed or highly anxious about life, talk to your doctor. Depression is no longer considered a moral or spiritual deficiency. In those discussions, be honest about your frustrations and emotions so the proper medications may be prescribed.

Remember that faith in God is relatively easy; there is actually a lot of evidence that He exists. Faith that everything will turn out well for you is a more difficult faith to sustain, but it is what having faith actually means. If you are still anxious about the risks of COVID-19 or the Second Coming, re-read the promises of the scriptures regarding the righteous. Once again, you know how this story of earth life ends. Granted, you don't know the individual path you will need to take to its end. But God has cared for your life up until now. You have the testimonies of friends and family and the promises in the scriptures. If you have anxieties about your future, your spiritual self needs to provide reassurance to your conscious mind that all will be well. Your conscious mind must take your spiritual self at its word and be comforted that the end of your story is known. Your mind and your spirit must rely on one another and strengthen each other. In the end, all will be well.

As a people, we want to get past the point where we are only worrying about surviving the day. We want to clear our minds of worry, depression, emails, and social media posts so we can consider the mysteries of the universe. We will be delighted with what we find there. There is so much to learn about eternal life. It would be a shame to further delay our search for the joys and pure knowledge that are available to us. I can think of no better way to end this book than with that promise. "If thou shalt ask, thou shalt receive revelation upon revelation, knowledge upon knowledge, that thou mayest know the mysteries and peaceable things—that which bringeth joy, that which bringeth life eternal" (D&C 42:61). May God bless you in your journey.

ABOUT THE AUTHOR

Scott R. Frazer joined The Church of Jesus Christ of Latter-day Saints when he was nineteen years old and left on a Church mission to Mexico City a year later.

Upon his return to Colorado, he married his wife, Cheri, and then completed his doctorate degree in analytical chemistry. His work history includes research roles in a variety of industries, but his passion is understanding the interactions of science and religion.

Since joining the Church, Scott has studied the overlaps between religious beliefs, conclusions of science, and laws of nature. His books are written to help readers make sense of their earthly challenges from both a technical and a spiritual perspective.